Creative display & environment

MARGARET JACKSON

SERIES EDITOR – MARGARET MORGAN

Hodder & Stoughton

A MEMBER OF THE HODDER HEADLINE GROUP

D0620228

British Library Cataloguing in Publication Data

Jackson, Margaret
    Creative Display and Environment. – (Art
    & Design for Learning Series)
    I. Title II. Series
    372.5

    ISBN–0 340–57340–6

Impression number   10 9 8 7 6 5 4 3 2 1
Year   1998 1997 1996 1995 1994 1993

First published 1993

Typeset by Wearset, Boldon, Tyne and Wear
Printed in Great Britain for Hodder & Stoughton Educational,
a division of Hodder Headline Plc, Mill Road, Dunton Green,
Sevenoaks, Kent by Scotprint Ltd.

Contents

Series preface: art and design for learning

Art and design for learning is a series of books which aims to provide a number of individuals involved in teaching with a platform from which to write about working with children and the thinking which lies behind their work.

The series authors are all experienced teachers and educationalists. They have had the privilege of visiting and working in schools, or of working with groups of teachers who have generously given permission for their children's work, and some of their own thoughts, to be included.

In the present climate of intense curriculum development created by the introduction of the National Curriculum for England and Wales, there is a great fear amongst some teachers that room for individuality and inventiveness is in danger of being lost. If this were to be the case, it would of course be disastrous but it need not happen.

Research historians and cooks experimenting with fifteenth- and seventeenth-century bread and cake recipes encountered failure until they realised that the key ingredient was never listed. This was because all the practitioners knew it to be such a basic necessity that everyone concerned would already know about it. The unlisted ingredient was yeast.

The same principle could be applied to many of our curriculum documents. The yeast in art and design education must surely be the life, energy and individuality of the child and the teacher, working creatively with the ingredient of experience and the means. Any defined curriculum agreed upon by others and presented to an establishment, an authority, county or state is inclined to appear restrictive at first glance, especially if we personally have not been responsible for drafting it. What we are able to do with it will depend on whether we see it as a platform to work from, or a cage to be imprisoned in.

It is therefore very important to coolly appraise the nature and content of the work we are undertaking with the children in our schools and to think carefully about our personal philosophy and values. We need to identify areas of any imposed curriculum that we are in fact already covering and then consider those which call for development or may need to be introduced. It is only when we really understand the common denominator which lies behind these areas of experience that we can assimilate them into a holistic and coherent developmental pattern on which to base our strategies for practice.

In simple terms any sound curriculum pertaining to art, craft and design must surely require a broad, balanced, developmental programme which has coherence and respects the experience, strengths, and weaknesses of individual children thereby enabling them to think, respond and act for themselves. Perhaps the real evaluation of a good teacher is to see whether children can proceed with their learning independently when he/she is no longer responsible for them.

The curriculum should make it possible to introduce children to the wonders and realities of the world in which we all live and should include art, craft and design forms from our own and other cultures and times. These can prove to be an enriching experience and can broaden the children's expectation of the nature of human response together with some experience of different ways of making art and design forms.

The curriculum should enable children to see the potential, and master the practice, of any relevant technologies: from the handling of simple hand tools to the world of information technology. It should enable them to work confidently in group and class situations as well as individually: thinking, making, appraising and modifying the work they are undertaking, negotiating skilfully with one another and discussing or talking about what they are doing, or have done. All of these aspects of education can be seen in the context of the National Curriculum which has, in the main, been based on some of the best practices and experience of work in recent years.

Intimations of the yeast component are clearly apparent in these selected extracts from *Attainment Targets and Programmes of Study for Key Stages 1 and 2*. (It is also very interesting to note the clear differences in requirements between the two stages; at seven- and at eleven-years-of-age. Stage 2 assimilates and develops Stage 1 requirements, building on them developmentally with specific additions.) At Key Stage 1 (seven-years) the operative words are:

> **investigating, making, observing, remembering, imagining, recording, exploring, responding, collecting, selecting, sorting, recreating, recognising, identifying, *beginning* to make connections ... [my italics].**

There is a very strong emphasis throughout on *direct experience*, *looking at* and *talking about*. At Key Stage 2 (eleven-years) the following expectations are added:

> **communicating ideas and feelings, developing ideas, experimenting [there is a subtle difference between exploration and conscious experimentation], applying knowledge, planning and making, choosing appropriate materials, adapting and modifying, comparing, looking for purposes, discussing ...**

What could be clearer in suggesting a lively educational experience? I believe that individuality and inventiveness are firmly based on having the right attitudes and they usually thrive best in the context of vehicles such as interest, happenings and the building up of enthusiasm and powerful motivation. The overall structure, balance and developmental nature of any sound curriculum model can allow content to flourish in lively interaction between children, teachers and the world of learning experiences.

If we persist in hardening the content of the National Curriculum in such a way that we are not able to manoeuvre or respond to the living moment, then we have ourselves forged the links of the chain which binds us.

The books in this series do not aim to be comprehensive statements about particular areas of art, craft and design experience but they are vigorous attempts to communicate something of the personal, convinced practice of a number of enthusiastic professionals. We hope that they will also offer enough information and guidance for others to use some of the approaches as springboards for their own exploration and experience in the classroom.

Margaret Morgan, Series Editor and Art Education Consultant

But Miss! He is ever so friendly—
I thought you'd like him for the display!

She has just been asked to
take responsibility for display!

Preface

> The mind and senses need to be fed and nourished as much as the physical body, except that 'food' is all kinds of sensory – especially visual and tactile – imaginative and inventive experiences . . . If education is to mean anything it should be able to offer more than the random experiences picked up out of school. At least schools should offer different, perhaps more considered and thought out experiences to enable children to grow and progress in their development.
> (Keith Gentle, 1985)

Creative display and environment is a response to the implications of the National Curriculum which firmly stresses children's need for firsthand experiences. What stronger, firsthand learning resource can there be, than the very place in which we work, which provides nourishment to support our other experiences, and is a workshop for physical and mental practice?

The two main areas which this book explores are the whole-school and classroom environment and any part of the natural or made world which can be brought into it, including supportive techniques and human guidance.

Margaret Jackson has taught in a number of schools and has been responsible for leading teams of teachers to consider the importance of environment, visual communication and display. The schools Margaret taught in were notable for the quality of their learning environments which you could not fail to detect upon entering the buildings. Clearly, the headteacher, teachers and ancilliary staff were all thoroughly involved in a whole-school policy and practice which allowed interesting educational events to happen. These schools were inviting (they even smelled good!) and you were aware of a wealth of children's work of all kinds, presented simply and effectively together with foyer, corridor, hall and classroom resource displays which were all accessible and inviting. Not surprisingly Margaret was quickly invited to share her expertise with teachers in other schools and to lead sessions at Teacher and Professional Development Centres.

The environment in which we teach our children matters: it has to be home, resource centre, workshop and gallery all in one, because children are enabled or debilitated by being in it. It is a functional place and perhaps because of that it has failed for too long to attract the depth of thought and whole-school policy-making which it deserves. If we have not already done so we need to focus on this area of our hidden curriculum and develop it to its full potential.

The statutory requirements and programmes of study for the National Curriculum in England and Wales, Key Stages 1 and 2, make some very definite demands in regard to 'firsthand observation [and] exploration [of the] elements of art' – line, colour, tone, texture, pattern shape, form and space. The National Curriculum also requires recognition of different kinds of art, craft and design and that the children 'should make connections between their own work and that of other artists'.

What better way could there be to achieve these requirements than to be able to look about you and find that you are inhabiting an environment full of potential learning experience planned to achieve these very ends? The environment for research would be there, as would the opportunity to stand back from your own and your peers' work and to thoughtfully discuss, appraise and develop it.

There is a wide selection of environments and displays from many schools, presented in this book. All of them are existing working environments and have not been set-up for the occasion. They have all been used by children and teachers and are an integral part of the potential for learning in their schools and it is hoped that these will provide the reader with a wealth of valuable educational practice.

It is also hoped that the technical considerations and the ideas and guidance sections contained in this book, will offer teachers the necessary insights into basic know-how in regard to techniques and procedures for displays and a good learning environment and will give those who need it, confidence to develop their own practice in the schools in which they work.

Margaret Morgan, Art Education Consultant

Acknowledgments

I would like to thank the following teachers and headteachers for being so generous in loaning material and allowing me to photograph displays within their schools:

Ann Taylor; Jill Wright; Duncan Allen; Elaine Elliot; Elaine Nason; Douglas Gosling; Gary Mayes; Rob Brand; Mary-Anne Parke; Cedric Hinchliffe; Gill Riley; Val Nelson; Derek Roberts; Phillippa Thorpe and Fred Sedgwick. Thanks also to Mrs J. Wadlow, Neil Turner and Shirley Crosbie for their help in producing the material on Special Education. To Keith Gentle, thanks for allowing me to use extracts from his book *Children and Art Teaching*.

My grateful thanks also to Ray Petty, County Art and Design Adviser for Suffolk; Norman Manners, Senior County Art Adviser for Norfolk; and Tim Wilson, Advisory Teacher for Art and Design for Suffolk: for the loan of material from their resource collections.

Many thanks also to Margaret Morgan, Art Education Consultant, who gave support, advice, material encouragement and sustenance when I most needed it, and to Surinder and Roland Warboys, whose stained glass work is a constant inspiration to pupils, staff and visitors to Tattingstone C.P. School, Ipswich.

I am also very grateful to teachers and children from the following Suffolk schools whose work and/or environment is represented in this book: Beccles Middle School; Bungay Middle School; Claydon High School; Laxfield, All Saints C.E.V.C.P. School; Nacton C.E.V.C.P. School; Roman Hill Middle School; Tattingstone C.E.V.C.P. School; Whitton County Primary School; Wickham Market County Primary School; and Glenwood School in Bedfordshire.

I have taken care to include all the people who have been so helpful to me, but wish to apologise if, inadvertantly, anyone has been left out.

I dedicate this book to past and present staff and pupils of Beccles Middle School, with whom I share some wonderful memories of school life.

1 A pressing need: why display and environment for learning matter

INTRODUCTION

This book is designed to help teachers fulfil a pressing need in our education system, which has been highlighted by recent curriculum developments and which can be subdivided into two separate but interconnecting areas.

The first of these is the need to provide children with firsthand experience, using objects and items, natural and made, as stimuli for a wide range of learning experiences. The second is to provide a sound, practical and interesting environment in which education can effectively take place. I will start with the first of these areas.

I have always been aware of the power of real experiences and objects as a stimulus for learning. It was evident to me from early in my teaching career, that work of all kinds which grew from firsthand experience and which was unfettered by subject boundaries, had a vigour, depth, quality and value which far exceeded second-hand, purely verbal or descriptive approaches. What was more, the children seemed involved in a different way: the deeper they delved, the deeper there was to delve, and they developed an attitude in which a continuing search (rather than a single, finished end-product), began to be their aim. This was also the beginning of an understanding on my part, of the value of process rather than isolated end-products. The fact that children's concentration spans were constantly greater when working in this way was also an eye-opening realisation.

The second area is equally important. I have always felt that the environment in which learning takes place is of supreme importance in enriching the quality of the experience. A classroom, or school, is a very specialised place with a specialised purpose and it must be able to serve that purpose whatever its physical drawbacks may be. It must house children, staff and resources in a way which allows them to live, learn and function together in the most effective way possible. These two interconnected areas comprise one of the most important, yet neglected, issues facing schools today.

Children spend a long time within the education system, and a high percentage of that time is spent in the school. It is often said that in adult life we remember very little of our schooling and yet when asked, most people can visually recall incidents, environments and events. How important it is then, that we make these visual memories positive ones.

Impressions made in childhood are often with us for life, therefore children should be encouraged to share in the organisation and development of their environment. Children often have very definite ideas, with strong likes and dislikes, sometimes without understanding why they feel so strongly. By discussion and by working together, they can learn to develop ideas, to compromise (one of the most important lessons we can teach them), to understand, progress and find solutions to practical problems concerning their immediate environment and other wider issues.

Some authorities say that at least 60 per cent of learning takes place through visual and tactile experiences and responses through the senses. It is therefore vital that we should instil the wish to explore and investigate by creating exciting, attractive and practical environments in which children can work, play and learn. The school and classroom should offer stimulating and supportive resources, materials and tools. It must have places for children to work individually and in groups, to research, relax, eat and play. We can be sure that the whole ambience of our classroom and school will undoubtedly affect the way in which they apply themselves and the values they come to accept.

It is also possible that when children (like adults), cease to care about their environment, or feel detached from it, we are faced with additional social problems such as thoughtlessness, litter and even vandalism. Surely children who feel responsible for and value their surroundings, are more likely to care for it.

I have been particularly aware of the issue of the hidden curriculum when looking at the ambience and environment of a school, together with that most important yet unsung resource: the teacher! Whatever the qualities of the school building, its equipment and materials, without the committed, enthusiastic teacher all is lost! Enthusiasm and vision are catching and children soon reflect the amount of interest shown in them. If their work is respected and cared for, they will in turn respond in an increasingly positive way.

If children's work is accepted and valued, discussed, mounted, displayed and stored safely, their self-respect will also be built-up.

Likewise, if corridors and common areas are inviting, with interesting, well-presented resources, the school ethos can draw both the visitor and those working in the school, into a pleasurable celebration of all kinds of learning. Display is not window dressing, it is the basis of a very real part of education. It can offer the stimulation to think, to research, to create, to experiment and design.

When children's work is presented there is also an opportunity for them to look at it and appraise it, seeing it not only as the culmination of earlier processes but also as an important springboard for further developments or new avenues of thought and action.

As teachers we can never be too visually aware and we need to understand how we all learn through touching and seeing, for this is a primary skill which needs to be constantly developed. It is interesting to consider to what extent any of us really see and what messages and standards we convey to our children by means of our organisation of space and resources.

The whole-school environment should offer opportunities for learning through displays of resource materials and children's work, in many cases showing interaction between the two. It is a means of communication which can stimulate thinking, creativity, aesthetic learning and cross-fertilisation of ideas. It can also support the development of life skills, encouraging children to observe, study, analyse and research, as well as enabling them to process visual information from diagrams, maps, charts and posters.

Children should also be encouraged to broaden their experience by being introduced through the use of display, to a wide variety of original works of art, design forms and reproductions. Looking at expressive and functional qualities in other people's art and design and considering shape, form, pattern, space, colour, line, tone and texture (all the elements of art) helps to make the children's own work more real and relevant.

There needs to be a build-up of all manner of experiences and learning through the vehicle of visual communication and display. The items and their qualities, appropriate and clearly presented information and the care shown by the teacher will all have an educational value, whilst the steady build up of discriminatory skills is also being encouraged and developed in the child. Children can, however, only learn discrimination when they have experienced enough to discriminate with. In discussing different criteria for judgement, children readily involve themselves in discerning quality and qualities.

It is specially important for children with learning difficulties to be surrounded by resources which make the most of their sensory faculties. In fact many special school units have developed this mode of learning to a high degree, with visual, tactile and sound components playing a vital educational role.

This entire area of display and environment for learning, requires a whole-school policy to be effective. We have to think about all aspects of school life as interrelated; no longer can display and environment be seen as solely the business of the art teacher. We are all aware of the psychology of advertising and visual manipulation and the degree to which we are all influenced in our daily lives by the presentation of this kind of material. We are met on all sides by advertising, shop displays, films and videos, the written word, exhibitions, museums and galleries and many other visual experiences, and yet surrounded as we are in the high street and our homes by visual display and communication, how is it we have neglected it for so long in our schools? It is also useful to consider the means by which good and bad communication skills are attained, children always enjoy this kind of discussion and it gets right to the heart of the issue. Surely, surrounded by high-quality visual displays, it would be much easier for our children to attain such skills.

Another important issue is that learning environments can play a strong part in developing links between educational disciplines. Often a number of ways of learning can grow from a common theme and the addition of children's own work to the initial stimuli can develop it still further and show a natural interaction of subject areas. (See the curricular flow charts on pages 60–61.)

Design and information technology will also be found to be relevant in the context of visual communication and display. It helps children to understand sequences and processes if a working progression is displayed showing clear developments from single idea to completed project. For example a presentation or display on the making of a toy would include initial designs (including computer design), choice of suitable materials, tools, stages of making, modifications, end-product, notes on the progression and evaluation.

To conclude this introductory section let us look at what the National Curriculum has to say about visual input in our schools:

Visual understanding deepens aesthetic responsiveness as no other mode of learning can, by enhancing the imagination and intensifying feelings, ideas and sensitivities.

STRATEGY FOR STAFF DEVELOPMENT

It is imperative that we develop our use of display and our school environment as far as we can, but how should we do it?

It is useful to think about the school as a whole and to consider the impression it creates. The staff will need to agree to work as a team and consider their own experience, skills and strengths to decide where particular help is necessary and who can fulfil specific needs.

The following strategy could well be adopted as the first stage of a plan for developing this whole area of experience.

The following strategy could well be adopted as the first stage of a plan for developing this whole area of experience.

- Discuss the reasons for presentation and display and the potential effect that the environment has on staff and children.
- Take a fresh look at the whole school from:
  - the child's point of view;
  - the teacher's point of view;
  - the visitor's point of view.

What messages are we sending in regard to the liveliness and quality of the education we offer? This may well lead to a plan for specific areas of the school to be developed, including key areas for resource display sites. These can be costed and put onto a rolling programme as finance allows.

- Discuss the possibility of building a resource bank and consider appropriate storage and organisation of these resources.
- Divide up responsibility for particular areas of the school amongst the staff. This may well require shared responsibility for certain central public areas.
- Timetable periodic discussion and appraisal of developments.
- Set-up in-service workshops for staff to build up skills in practical design, arrangement and display and lettering (by hand, word processor or other means such as Letraset or stencils).

Once the staff have been persuaded of the value of a whole-school policy on environment and display for learning and areas of the school have been targeted for development, the next stage outlines some central points to be considered in surveying the school.

Figure 1(a)

Figure 1(b)

Figure 1(a,b,c) (Continued overleaf) The fact that part of this primary school is in the old school house does not deter teachers and pupils from displaying their work as a celebration of learning. Every space is used sensitively to create environments for all to enjoy

Figure 1(c)

POINTS TO CONSIDER WHEN SURVEYING THE SCHOOL

- Begin by looking at possibilities for developing the main entrance.
- Look at possibilities for developing other entrance areas. What potential do they have? What impact could be created? I have seen dark, dismal entrances transformed by a change of colour and strategically placed lighting in order to enhance learning resources and children's work.
- Select particular sites for development rather than thinking about end-to-end display areas throughout the school.
- Look for potential wall-board areas. These can be very simple, unframed, fire-proof pin-boards fixed to the walls. They will have far greater potential if they cover as wide an area as possible rather than constituting a single, narrow board.
- Look for areas which could be used for children's group work for example murals, large paintings, collages, textile hangings, ceramics, freestanding sculptural forms etc.
- Select promising vistas, for instance looking down a corridor to a display on the end wall can be very effective. Such an end wall lends itself to displaying large items.
- Don't forget the outside environment: playgrounds, outside walls, gardens, nature areas. (See figure C2(c) on page 98 in the colour section.)

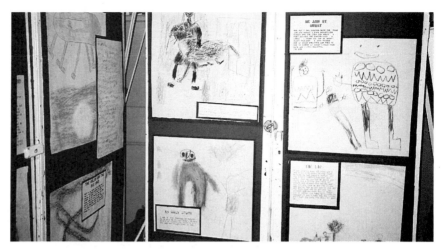

Figure 2   Cupboard doors have been utilised as display surfaces to exhibit reception children's work

Figure 3   Adjustable shelving fitted into a window recess to create a display setting. This is particularly appropriate for translucent objects

Figure 4   A play area, built with the co-operation of parents and friends of the school helps to make the playground a more exciting place to be

Figure 5   It is important to look at the exterior environment as a means of developing ideas, enthusiasm, skills and knowledge. This small garden area has many interesting facets, including a vegetable section

Figure 6 · A mural painted on what was a plain wall, transforming the area into a colourful and exciting environment. This was produced in liaison with high school pupils

Figure 7 Small panels or walls can be made with stones which the children have collected to add interest and texture to an outside environment

21

Figure 8 Furniture and plants arranged as silhouettes against a window

Looking at areas of the school with an eye to displaying their own material can be a valuable exercise for children, as it allows them to develop projects both creatively and practically and is a first rate 'design for purpose' brief. Planned well, it is possible to include most curriculum areas and this activity can involve children in all kinds of decision making. It is amazing what a bit of paint, carpet, some seating and trees and plants can do and if there isn't enough money in the school fund to buy new materials, it is always worth asking the parent–teacher group if it can help. In fact there are very often items of old furniture such as tables, lockers and benches which can make excellent display units when refurbished or covered, at little or no cost. Covered tins or boxes can also be used as stands (see page 78).

Spring and autumn are good times to ask for plant cuttings and seeds. A well-worded letter to local businesses often reaps wonderful rewards, sometimes in unexpected ways. I have been offered items ranging from a foot pump to a gold bra display bust!

INVOLVING CHILDREN IN THE CREATION OF A LEARNING ENVIRONMENT

The issue of children's involvement in education through display and environment is a critical one. Obviously, there are situations where adults alone may take the initiative, with the teacher in particular playing a major part. However some very interesting displays are set up in schools by parents, visitors, and ancillary staff.

Figure 9 Plants and interesting containers always brighten up an area

On the other hand, there are exhibitions where children are fully involved and on some occasions they take full responsibility for the entire project. Clearly the recurring, day-to-day interaction of child with materials and challenges is the main purpose of presentation and the development of the display. Even very young children can get involved as they enjoy selecting and arranging things. Many of us will be able to remember enjoying playing at 'shops' and arranging and rearranging our personal collections of seeds, flowers, marbles, toys, cards and other items. Many older children like to arrange their personal belongings and posters in their rooms. This is the interest and energy which we, as teachers, should build on.

Figure 10 Discussing and assessing work is an important part of the learning process. Here nursery children look at a display of paintings with their teacher

Figure 11 A classroom where children learn to develop organisational skills by experiencing, and working with, materials and equipment which are well managed

Likewise as soon as children can write they will enjoy labelling things, and they will recognise the potential and interest in presenting and displaying work if the ambience of the school communicates the value of such activities to them.

When a major project is being considered, discussing the subject matter and possible strategies with the children can lead to valuable initiatives and often generates good ideas. (See figures 12a, b and c.) Children are involved from the beginning and if the teacher is enthusiastic they will enjoy contributing ideas and collecting items to add to the display. These, it must be said, are not always appropriate or even welcome but it is important to receive the item graciously, discussing the criteria for selection and sometimes deciding that it needs another 'home' where it can be seen and enjoyed for whatever qualities it displays! The most important thing is that the child is involved enough to bring something and should not be discouraged from doing so again.

Figure 12(a,b,c)   These three panels (above and opposite) show work which has been based on particular projects, and which has entailed co-operation, planning and practice

You can find out about the space-bat-angel-dragon if you read The Iron Man.

It is possible for children to work on displays alone, in pairs, or in groups and to select items based on a chosen theme. These collections excite much discussion as they are built-up and usually cause great interest amongst those not currently involved in the making of that particular display.

Learning display skills

Children do need to be explicitly taught some of the techniques involved, although none of these skills are only specific to display. Cutting can be introduced as a lesson, or a series of lessons, as the

Figure 13(a)

Figure 13(a,b,c) Involving children in the organisation of their work areas and equipment is important. Cleaning equipment or tidying away materials into boxes is a means of introducing and developing the practical and organisational skills which are so necessary in later life

Figure 13(b)

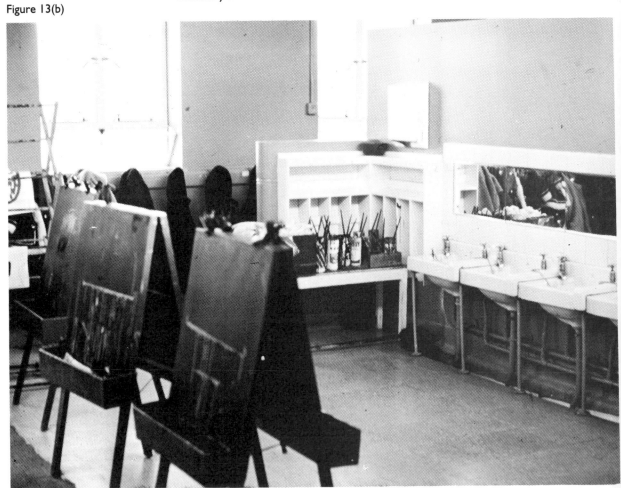

Figure 13(c)

children mature and can handle more complex modes of working. Other tools should also be carefully introduced and the children taught to respect them. To offer children scissors, for instance, which are so blunt that they will not function on the grounds of health and safety would be a mistake. It is difficult enough for an adult to use these safe, blunt scissors and it will therefore be impossible for a child to do so. Safety, of course, should be carefully discussed but the purpose of a pair of scissors is to cut and children should simply be taught to treat them cautiously.

Similarly the use of adhesives requires specific practice and should be introduced only after the teacher and children have talked about solvents and their inherent dangers. One might ask is this art or science? It is, of course, both. A practical session which involves the challenge to enjoy collaging materials and to see how little glue they can use and still make the items stick is a useful way into a deeper analysis of the scientific properties of materials as well as an understanding of the aesthetic values necessary for display. Using different materials requiring a variety of glues as in a collage, or in a sculptural form made from boxes, tins and other found objects, is also a useful technical experience. It is interesting to get children to time the drying properties of different adhesives. Discussion of their findings and the suitability of the various glues tried is an important part of this experience.

SUMMARY

Displays themselves can be either a short-term celebratory experience or something which is kept in the classroom or school to be used and developed. This involves skills such as labelling, notetaking, creative or descriptive writing, painting, modelling and the skill of adding appropriate information books. In this way displays become ongoing experiences and may be built-up and used in the same way as any other major resource. I have seen displays which include miniature gardens, transport models, flowers, sports equipment, clothing, photographs and transluscent objects to name but a few of the vast array of display items which children, once guided and encouraged, can use to improve their learning environment whilst exploring themes and ideas which cross all subject boundaries.

2 Displays and the art of displaying

INTRODUCTION

The word 'display' sometimes creates near panic in some circles. People often feel that they need highly specialised skills and techniques which they do not possess! Yet interesting and useful learning environments may be achieved in many ways and without requiring the enormous amount of effort that instils fear into the hearts of inexperienced displayers.

The most important thing to consider is the function of the display and the creation of a simple layout which will allow each component object to be seen clearly in its own right, or in relation to others. You do not have to cover the whole school with mountains of double and triple mounted pictures, writing, posters or mobiles to achieve an interesting effect. That clearly would be a poor use of time and energy. It is, however, often valuable to have isolated areas of colour or texture which are there simply as a complement to the work or resource, allowing them to be seen more effectively.

Figure 14   Glove-and-rod puppets grouped on draped fabric. Each can be seen clearly as they are spaced sensitively on a simple background

Figure 15(a)

Figure 15(b)

Figure 15(d)

Figure 15(a,b,c,d)   Positive and negative forms, illustrating the importance of space in relation to the shape

Figure 15(c)

Colour plays an important part in the general impression and feel of a building. Dark areas need light colours. Cold areas, warm colours and consideration should be given to the linking of separate areas by using colour. One should aim for a bright, cheerful and clean atmosphere where it is a pleasure to work.

Considering space is also absolutely vital when creating any environment, regardless of the scale. The balance of an object or picture with it's surroundings should be such that relevant information is seen and the overall effect attracts the eye and interests the viewer (see figures 14, 15a, b, c and d and 16a and b). The negative (unused) space has to be as important as the positive object if it is to be seen to its best advantage.

In order to create a good educational environment I have always tried to display materials without suggesting clutter and without producing an oppressive atmosphere, always remembering that many of the display items needed to be handled and used and therefore had to be easily accessible.

Figure 16(a) Silhouette portraits drawn and cut out by children, then used as a mount or frame for their written work

Figure 16(b) Silhouette forms glued on to cellophane and displayed in front of a window to achieve maximum impact

DISPLAY VARIATIONS

Display can take many forms and fulfil many functions. Those listed below represent the major types, but it is not an exhaustive list. In practice there will be considerable overlap and growth and development from one form to another. Items and artefacts can have different purposes and meanings depending on the context in which they are set and the way in which the teacher chooses to use them. For example musical instruments could be included in a science display on sound, for analytical drawing in art, or as a stimulus for creative writing, as well as for reference for a curriculum-based display on music.

- Informative displays – displayed on notice boards for example, sports results and fixtures, library information, school activities, clubs (see figures 17a, b and c overleaf).
- Curriculum area displays – humanities: displays of artefacts from a given area, era or culture. Maths: displays illustrating area, surface, shapes, solids and patterns. English: displays including books, book covers, poetry and styles of lettering. Music: displays of various instruments, record sleeves and pictures of famous musicians. Science: display items such as natural forms, colour, light, food and space.
- Creative and imaginative displays – using natural resources and created artefacts (see figure 23 on pages 46–9) to stimulate ideas for development of language, creative writing, art and design technology.
- Practical displays – to demonstrate anything from processes and relationships of materials, through to industrial and commercial links.
- Children's work – displayed to communicate research, recording, reporting, communicating, celebrating acquired knowledge, feelings and responses to curriculum studies (see figures 18a, b, c, d, and e on pages 33–4).

Figure 17(a)

Figure 17(b)

Figure 17(c)

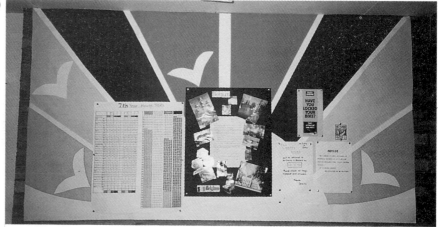

Figure 17(a,b,c) Notice boards need to be particularly well organised. Areas
can be sectioned off with tape or paper strips and headings should be clearly printed.
Sometimes blocks of colour used as backgrounds help to draw attention to the board

Figure 18(a)

Figure 18(a,b)   (above) Giant masks made for a school production in foam, paper and polystyrene. They sit neatly in an alcove, adding new dimensions to the classroom

Figure 18(c)   A young child's response to a museum visit. The display shows how much the work is valued

Figure 18(d)   Wall space is gallery space

Figure 18(e)   A primary classroom where work and resources are displayed and used to the fullest extent

The variety of display combines to enhance the stimulating and ongoing learning process in the school environment. One of the most valuable aspects of all categories of display is that they enable children to see their own work as it proceeds. Instant presentations are particularly pertinent when we are asking children to assess their own work (see figures 20a, b and c on pages 36 and 37). They can be easily organised at the end of a lesson, and it is quite exciting for children to see their contribution laid out on the floor, well spaced, and preferably placed on appropriate mounting paper, or alternatively pegged out in a line at eye level. This encourages children to step back and view their work from a distance or from a different angle and encourages them to be aware of visual impact. It enables them to make judgements in the light of their original intentions, or with an eye to a particular problem set, or solved, which leads to discussion and evaluation.

Within the classroom one should also allow for instant display when resources are brought together to support a lesson, or items of news. They may consist of things which can only be used for short periods, such as perishable goods, or something brought from home.

Figure 19(a)

Figure 19(c)

Figure 19(b)

Figure 19(a,b,c)   These three figures show small areas of classrooms which have been put aside for immediate display of information such as postcards or children's own work. The spaces are used to pin-up work as it progresses, or choose, use, and replace cards at random as and when information is needed

Figure 20(a)

Figure 20(b)

Figure 20(a,b)   Children selecting suitable mounting paper for their work

Figure 20(c) An instant exhibition, where work is placed on sugar paper or a similar material, enabling children to stand back and assess their pictures

These are just as valuable in their own way as the longer standing displays. Children should be encouraged to bring items into school and to organise and arrange them in order to develop ideas and facilitate knowledge, understanding of balance, scale, shape, form, space, colour and tone, through practical involvement, discussion, observation, questioning and activity making.

Suspended displays

One type of display which could fall under a number of the general categories listed previously are suspended displays. The possibilities for these will depend very much on the physical design of the school. Some buildings lend themselves to this, while others clearly do not! Older buildings often have the advantage of exposed beams or metal rods and piping which can be effectively utilised. There is something very exciting to young children about suspended objects, particularly moving ones. A suspended display can positively utilise an otherwise unused area of space, whilst the experience of looking up to an ever-changing mobile or hanging and seeing different components, changing space-shapes and shadows, is always interesting. To create suspended displays it will be necessary first of all to fix permanent rods, batons, cord, wire-lines, or hooks at various points so that items can be attached to them. It is possible to arrange a pulley system which will enable the display to be raised and lowered at will. Another alternative is to suspend a fishing net or something similar across the room, and peg, clip, or tie items on to it. This can also be done with a spreading tree branch.

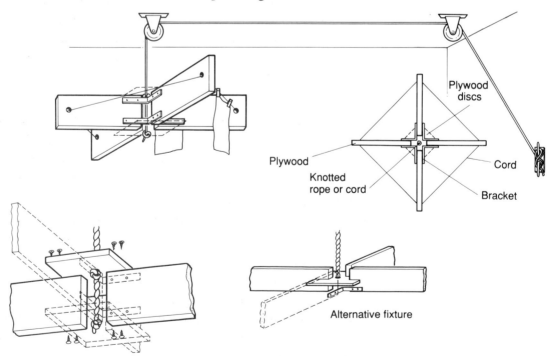

Figure 21   Pulley system for displaying or drying work

These systems will take some effort to install, but once in position they can be semi-permanent fixtures if that is what is required. It is possible to purchase suspension equipment from a number of educational stockists if you do not wish to make your own. Of course, we need to be aware of fire hazards and particular attention should be paid to choosing suitable materials and considering suitable sites.

Group work murals and large wall-hangings

Another type of display which can fall under a number of categories mentioned previously is the mural. I have been very impressed by the many imaginative ways which have been devised in some schools to involve children in interesting educational activities and at the same time bring their learning environments to life. This was particularly true in some of the older buildings which offered teachers a daunting challenge. Murals often played a large part in enhancing the learning environment in some of these schools.

Creating a mural or wall-painting can offer a great wealth of experience to children: there are new challenges in relation to scale, in considering interesting subject matter and in utilising a particular space. Before considering their responses to the challenge and before making decisions about the content and ways in which they are going to work, children should always be encouraged to see and discuss the actual place where their work will be mounted.

Pictures painted directly on to walls will, with some exceptions, need careful planning beforehand. This planning can be seen as an important part of the learning process. Alternatively, panels can be made from hardboard or other surface sheeting and put in place by means of batons or rawl plugs. The advantage of this method is that it enables children to work at floor level and allows for easy removal of the old picture when a new painting is required. (A coat of emulsion will cover the surface prior to new work commencing.)

Young children may need some encouragement before working on a large scale but by allowing them to experiment freely on large pieces of newsprint or pieces of paper joined together, they soon gain confidence. Older children can be taught to scale-up their designs, or to use the old-fashioned but still useful epidiascope to reproduce their own designs on a larger scale, by transposing them on to a suitable surface. Teachers should not be tempted to undertake the initial drawing for the children as this defeats the whole purpose of the exercise and takes the challenge out of it.

Murals can be produced as a whole or in sections both on the exterior and interior of buildings. Children love working on a large scale when they get used to it and there is something magical about a wall displaying a large piece of group work. I have also visited primary schools where local high school pupils had been invited to work with younger children on such a project. This can be a wonderful exercise in liaison and an opportunity for different age groups to work together (see figure 6 on page 21).

Group work with murals can, of course, take many forms. For example a series of paintings the same size can be pieced together to form a composite picture, or a frieze. Similarly a large weaving or ceramic wall panel which a number of children have worked on (or a group of individual designs which are grouped together to form a whole), can be created and hung on a wall to create a large-scale wall-hanging. Collages are also popular where the individual parts are made by the children and then co-ordinated by them on to a background (see figure 24a, b and c on pages 50–51).

Material suitable for murals and large wall-hangings
Many kinds of materials are suitable for large wall-hangings and murals and one need not be limited by this form. If the mural is to be painted, powder, emulsion, or tempera paints can be used. Quite a number of partly used tins of paint may be offered by parents or friends of the school once it is known that they are required, although it is necessary to remember that outside murals must be weatherproof. It might also be worth approaching a local stockist, or better still a paint manufacturer if you have one in the area, to enquire about suitable paints. Play your cards right and you might even be given some end of colour ranges free of charge.

Besides paint, many other items can be utilised to create interesting murals or wall-hangings. Collections of threads, wools, fabrics, found objects and items such as wood, grasses, beads and seeds may all be incorporated into paintings, weavings or collages. If a durable surface is required, PVA or a similar glue will add strength and bonding to a surface. Murals can be designed to any shape or size to fit a particular area of the school.

Changing environments

Changing areas of the school – public places, corridors or classrooms – into display environments is rich in educational experience. For children to become part of a setting of this kind, surrounded by colour, texture and pattern, and being made aware of space and form is an experience in its own right. There are many examples of teachers working with children to transform their surroundings into jungles, spaceships, autumn landscapes, factories and many other environments. One school made caves from paper and corrugated card, into which the children crawled to paint the walls with their own paint made from natural materials such as berries, chalk, ground charcoal and root vegetables (see figure C7a and b on page 103).

In another school a project was undertaken where part of the classroom became a large tent, with fabrics suspended to create a huge awning, and eastern-style artefacts such as rugs, lamps and cushions were arranged within it. This was a wonderful environment in which pupils learnt something about other cultures. This type of lesson is surely a memorable and exciting way to educate children.

SUMMARY

Whatever type of display or environment-changing project is chosen, one of the most valuable aspects of working with such resources is the interest and growth of ideas which seem to be generated in the teams of teachers who work with them. Such resources spark ideas, and one thing leads to another. Children too become deeply involved, by responding to the stimulating arrangements. As we have seen, the content of the displays can be selected for its usefulness in developing particular curriculum or cross-curricular themes or can be purely artistic. Displays are developmental by their very nature and will change and grow as more items are added and as the children's own work on the project is added to the original source.

A good display thus acts as a catalyst in the hands of the enthusiastic teacher and has many of the resources for research and development built into it. Information which is needed can be searched for in the book corner or library, or by the children questioning adults at home. Whatever methods are chosen, displays are always an ongoing and highly educational experience.

3 Resources for display

ACQUIRING ARTEFACTS AND DESIGNED FORMS

A resource display is only as good as the material it exhibits, because children can only utilise a display effectively if it provides sufficient information and stimuli for them to develop ideas from it. Yet acquiring enough suitable artefacts and designed forms for a specific resource display can be something of a challenge.

Even when working as a team within the school, we found that we needed to use our combined initiatives as well as looking for support from children, parents, governors and industry and commerce. To provide our children with artefacts and designed forms relevant to specific topics and areas of particular interest necessitated advance planning.

When organising a project on the Second World War and how it affected the area in which our school was situated, we enlisted the help of the local paper to ask the public for relevant information and to appeal for any items of interest. Meanwhile the children interviewed older residents in the community and people connected with local businesses. Contacts were made with past pupils through old school records, including some people who had been evacuated to the area during the war. Local branches of the service organisations such as the Royal British Legion were also asked to contribute items and information.

The response was amazing. We received so much material that the display area had to be extended along the school corridors. People loaned us uniforms, gas masks, documents such as ration books and war records, medals, letters, photographs, old newspapers and many other relevant artefacts. We could have spent a whole year working from these resources.

In regard to collecting interesting items, clearly what a single person or small group can do, a larger group can do better! Encouraging the general public to join us is very much to our interest in this context. It is therefore useful to have a school resource list of possible contacts when specific kinds of items are required. For a display on machinery one may require objects ranging from a typewriter to a bicycle, and one would obviously request help from different sources depending on what was needed and where the emphasis of the display lay. Clearly the more contacts one has, the easier it usually is to acquire the information and artefacts one needs. This resource list is particularly invaluable for new members of staff. The short list below outlines some of the possible sources of help that one might try.

- Local industry and commerce are usually only too willing to supply waste or scrap materials free of charge as long as the materials are collected, sometimes on a regular basis.
- Letters to parents, governors and friends of the school are normally a good way of acquiring items.
- Advertisements in the local paper can also be very rewarding, although it is sometimes necessary to suggest lists of required items, as people do not always realise what can be utilised.
- Items needed for a particular project should be included in the school newsletter, well in advance of course.
- Some schools send a standard letter to parents and local businesses at regular intervals, with lists of items which are likely to be in constant use.

RESOURCE BANKS

Once a school has built-up a certain amount of display material the problem becomes one of storage. In order to store resources adequately it is necessary to organise a space into a resource area: a room, cupboard, or even a curtained recess, will do. This is a good idea because many items can be used time and again in a variety of ways and over a period of time the school collection will build up impressively.

It is important to make someone responsible for organising the care and storage of resources including those borrowed from staff, parents, museums and galleries and for items which may need relocating to different areas of the school or putting into temporary storage. There will, of course, always be a need for some forward-

and team-planning. Rushing down to the resources room at the last available moment to get the stuffed owl for your group's nature and poetry lesson only to find it has been borrowed by Mr Johnston to lighten his burden in maths, can be very irritating!

Obviously when creating a resource centre you cannot store an endless supply of artefacts, unless your school is fortunate enough to have large areas of unused space and I wonder if any one of us has yet met a headteacher who will admit to that! There are some items however, which are likely to be of value across the curriculum and which are reasonable easy to store when not in use. However, do not forget that most of your artefacts will be on display around the school almost continuously, being reused in various guises almost like objects in a travelling exhibition: therefore only a small number need be stored at any one time.

Natural and made objects for the resource bank

Natural objects are always useful to have around as interesting and informative material and they are easily collectable. Such items include:

Figure 22(a)   Items of interest displayed to create atmosphere in a small corner

- interesting stones – granite, slate, flint, pebbles, amber and jet;
- seaside collections – shells, dead starfish, seaweed and fossils;
- feathers – peacock, pheasant and duck;
- floral collection – dried grasses, flowers and twigs;
- wood offcuts – with prominent grains, such as elm, rosewood, oak and walnut;
- twisted roots and pieces of bark or logs with unusual patterns and shapes;
- look for interesting shape, colour and texture when choosing any of these items.

(See figures 23a, b, c, d, e, f, g, h and i on pages 46–9.)

There are a number of made artefacts which are also worth keeping on a permanent basis. These include:

- originals – works of art, craft and design;
- paper products – postcards, posters, photographs, calendars;
- mechanical objects – wheels, cogs, bits of interesting machinery, threads, bottles;
- packaging – such as boxes of different sizes and shapes and papers (there are some lovely wrapping paper designs based on natural, traditional and cultural themes for sale);
- larger objects – fishing nets, lobster pots, clocks, musical instruments and ceramics may be stored or borrowed for a limited period if storage is a problem.

Figure 22(b)
Collected natural objects and artefacts are always useful as sources for study, as well as for creative and imaginative work

The list is potentially endless: anything and everything is of educational value and should be considered as a means of stimulating interest and learning through display. Most of the materials in the list above could be stored quite easily as the basis of a permanent resource bank. Large, flat items such as posters, maps and pictures can be kept in plan-chests, paper storage areas, or rolled and kept in clean drums (try local manufacturers), or purpose-built folder boxes. Other small- to medium-sized artefacts may be kept in labelled sturdy boxes or trays. Keeping these in good condition could be a job either for the children or for a willing parent.

Figure 23(a)

Figure 23(a,b,c,d,e,f,g,h)   Resources play an important part in creating interesting environments. Collections of natural and made objects can be stored in trays or covered boxes, on shelves or on window sills to add interest to a room or area. Some large items may be suspended if there is little space

Figure 23(b)

Figure 23(d)

Figure 23(c)

Figure 23(e)

Figure 23(f)

Figure 23(g)

Figure 23(h)

Figure 23(i)   A relief panel and three-dimensional forms made from natural objects

ART GALLERIES, ARTISTS AND CRAFTSPEOPLE

Many art galleries are a very good source of supply for loans and gifts of display material. They sometimes offer free items, usually in the form of posters and catalogues. It is worth putting your school on the mailing list as galleries will continue to send you updated information on a regular basis once your school is known to them.

Books and postcards can also be purchased from galleries, museums and bookshops and are valuable resources. They are often available in sets, for example, schools of artists and designers, or themes such as landscape, trees, bridges, architecture, figures, abstracts, or particular design and craft categories. These sets can last for years if covered in plastic. (If your school does not own a plasticising machine, it is worth enquiring at your nearest high school, or teachers centre.) The same gallery shops are rich sources of reproduction pictures. They can be a very valuable resource, for often a display of postcards or posters can bring to life a specific

Figure 24(a)   Artist in residence, Liz Rideal (Education Officer at the National Portrait Gallery), working on a large-scale collage. Liz composes her work from small photographs, using a photo-booth and coloured gels. She was sponsored to work alongside children as part of a competition prize

educational experience or an aspect of a lesson. I have always found it invaluable to have immediate visual information available to enable discussion, comparison and questioning. It is also worth remembering that if the resources won't come to you, you can go to them, for most museums and galleries are happy for school parties to work on the premises under supervision. This is always a stimulating environment to take children into and has wonderful potential as a source of inspiration.

Artists and craftspeople may also be willing to involve themselves in projects, or lend work to schools. I know of examples where collections of work have been lent to schools and then passed on from school to school. This opens up tremendous possibilities for creative studies across the curriculum and would enable spaces such as libraries, foyers and communal areas to be developed as galleries where artists' originals, prints of famous paintings and children's work could be hung side by side.

Figure 24(b,c)   Children developing two of the three large-scale collages later displayed in an exhibition which celebrated their work

Figure 25(a) Nine-year-old children working with an epidiascope to enlarge their sketches on to a board

MUSEUMS

Like galleries, museums are a very good source of display materials, and are usually only too willing to help schools. Most have an education section, which will organise the loan of artefacts and related information free of charge in most cases. They also produce a range of items and educational packs suitable for a whole project. Visits to museums are of course invaluable resources in their own right.

Figure 25(b)   Children build up the picture into a tonal collage

BOOKS AND ILLUSTRATIVE RESOURCES

I am sure that anyone in education will agree that good quality, well-illustrated books are a most necessary resource for any subject area. The art, craft and design curriculum requires children to experience and learn from art and design forms, with the need for them to see examples of a wide range of fine art and functional items. There must be specific choices made to include books on fine arts and crafts but much information can be acquired from publications about other subject areas.

Humanities publications in particular have much to offer, as their content area covers a lot of highly visual material, such as ethnic artefacts, buildings and costume. Science publications too are very valuable as they include illustrations of plants and animals, highly-magnified pictures and photographs of constellations in space – all of which can be utilised in displays.

Figure 26(a,b,c)   One group of children worked with students from Lowestoft college in the style of Hockney. They used photographs of their residential activities as the source for their pictures

It is therefore vital that books and visual information should be easily available to children, not only in the library but as part of the support material for displays. Displays don't have to concentrate solely on information books either, children's story books, if carefully chosen, can offer a wide selection of very useful illustration in a variety of media. Children should also be made aware of the special areas where they can find reference books either in the library, classrooms or corridors. Many teachers create quiet corners to encourage and facilitate reading. The more attractive these are, the more the child will want to work there. Interesting book covers, posters and illustrations strategically placed will excite interest and enquiry.

As with other resources advance planning is necessary to allow for sharing and the ordering of books from the public library service. But to make limited resources go further many of the better quality magazines such as the *National Geographic, World Wildlife*, some of the weekend supplement publications, and art and design magazines also provide wonderful illustrations and photographs. As they are produced on good-quality paper which does not deteriorate they can be transformed into long-lasting resource material. Mounted on card and covered with clear, sticky-backed plastic, these will last for years and can be used as an individual or group resource without you having to worry about them being marked by paint as you would with books. Sets can be built-up and stored in various categories to facilitate the development of knowledge, understanding and the use of art and design forms.

4 Developing a curriculum-based display project

INTRODUCTION

All schools will undertake curriculum projects which successfully focus on subjects which cross discipline boundaries. At their best they can be educationally rich, bringing into play children's interest and enthusiasm and enabling learning through verbal and non-verbal means. In this chapter I have laid out a well-tried and effective strategy for developing curriculum-based display projects, followed by a list of possible themes or subjects which I found to be useful starting points for work.

STRATEGY FOR DEVELOPING A CURRICULUM-BASED DISPLAY PROJECT

- Staff discussion with regards to particular curriculum needs, culminating in a decision being made as to the theme or project.
- Staff pool their energies and resources for the initial stages by working out flow-diagrams and discussing ideas. This is the 'think-tank' stage.
- Children become involved in the discussion of the project. On occasions in the early stages this is not possible but it can be a very valuable educational experience.
- Staff order special books and artefacts from libraries and museum services and organise loans of items from other teachers, parents, children and elsewhere. Resource bank artefacts should also be collected and organised.
- Sites for the displays are then agreed upon by staff.
- The building-up of the basic display then occurs with children's involvement wherever possible. (It is sometimes a good idea to hold back some of the resources so that they can be added to the display at a later stage when the children's work has developed beyond the initial stages.

- Children are introduced to the project either as a whole school by a team of teachers, *or* individual teachers introduce their classes to the project and follow up a particular aspect of it.
- Work commences by means of research, discussion, a specific challenge, practical involvement and encouragement of children to develop their own thinking and working.
- This in turn is followed by children and staff negotiating ways forward: assessing, monitoring and evaluating work and by making changes and refinements where it is considered appropriate. The possibilities for new awareness and new thought amongst the children often grows quite naturally and, in turn, leads to fresh challenges.
- To finish-off, the work can be celebrated by a presentation in the form of an exhibition, performance, recording, changed environment or any other means of communication. This presentation could be for the class, the school, or it might include parents and outsiders.
- Finally the whole experience will need to be discussed and evaluated by staff and pupils.

THEMES AND IDEAS FOR CURRICULUM-BASED DISPLAY PROJECTS

The examples of themes outlined in the list overleaf are just a few of the many used in schools to good effect. A team of teachers in one school first considered possible areas of experience and resource and built-up a chart. It was then possible to select any theme listed as a way into the chosen work, or by a particular curriculum discipline. There are no right or wrong ways to proceed. It can be equally as valid to approach a project through the visual and tactile, as the functional: through art, design or technology, or by considering the humanities, science or language. The important thing is to make sure that the strength of a discipline is maintained in its own right, rather than being used as a weak servicing agent for other areas. This method of working enables children to see the relevance of a theme in relation to a number of curriculum areas.

- Elements: colour – pigment and light; line–tone, pattern, texture, shape, form and space.
- Qualities: shine/shining, reflections, textures.
- Seasons: winter, spring, summer, autumn.
- Festivals: Harvest, Christmas, Easter, Ramadan, Yom Kippur, Pesach or Passover, Chinese New Year, Diwali, Thanksgiving.
- Buildings and building materials: particular local buildings, or groups of buildings; wood, stone, fabrics, plastics, tools.
- Contrasts: night/day, dark/light, happy/sad.
- Minibeasts: insects and other small creatures.
- Holes and cavities.
- Growth.
- A particular period in time: cavemen, Egyptians, Greeks, Victorians, civil wars, world wars.
- Books.
- Letter forms.
- Hats.
- Clothes/costume.
- Transport: animals, carriages, bicycles, cars, trains, ships, airships, balloons, aeroplanes.
- Machines.

USING CURRICULUM DISPLAYS

Once a theme or learning resource display has been built-up there are many ways in which it can be used for effective learning.

In the first place it will be necessary to stimulate the children's interest and enthusiasm by introducing the material in an attractive fashion. Sensory learning – looking, listening, touching (and where appropriate tasting and smelling) – can be a very valuable experience. Thinking about the qualities of cold, heat, weight, texture and pattern will add to the notion that nothing should be taken for granted.

You could then go on to discuss how and where we might find out more about the contents of the display. Who ought we to question? What might we find in books? Where are the books kept? What kind of work is to be undertaken? We should then consider how we should set about researching, recording, undertaking practical work and considering presentations and what resources and materials we might need. In practice some of the work will result from direct teacher challenge and some will be the children's own ideas discussed and negotiated with the teacher.

Humanities project

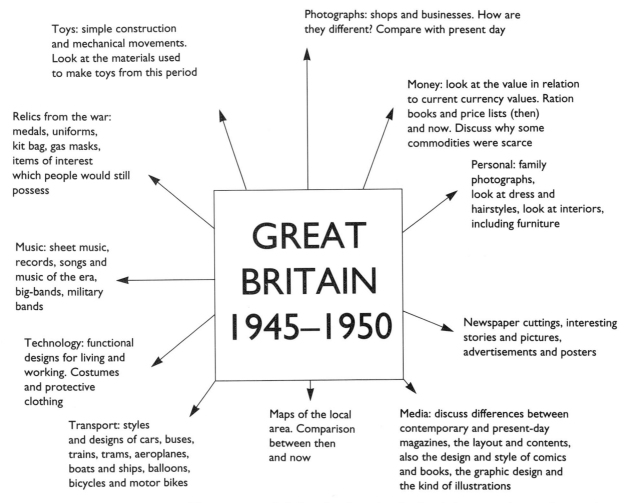

Toys: simple construction and mechanical movements. Look at the materials used to make toys from this period

Photographs: shops and businesses. How are they different? Compare with present day

Money: look at the value in relation to current currency values. Ration books and price lists (then) and now. Discuss why some commodities were scarce

Relics from the war: medals, uniforms, kit bag, gas masks, items of interest which people would still possess

Personal: family photographs, look at dress and hairstyles, look at interiors, including furniture

Music: sheet music, records, songs and music of the era, big-bands, military bands

GREAT BRITAIN 1945–1950

Newspaper cuttings, interesting stories and pictures, advertisements and posters

Technology: functional designs for living and working. Costumes and protective clothing

Transport: styles and designs of cars, buses, trains, trams, aeroplanes, boats and ships, balloons, bicycles and motor bikes

Maps of the local area. Comparison between then and now

Media: discuss differences between contemporary and present-day magazines, the layout and contents, also the design and style of comics and books, the graphic design and the kind of illustrations

There is a great deal of work to be undertaken in relating comparisons and contrasting artefacts and designed forms and values of the period to those of the present day

A project based on pictures would also allow different aspects of the National Curriculum to be explored either in isolation or as part of a curriculum-wide project – art, science, maths, music, history and language could all be accessed through this project.

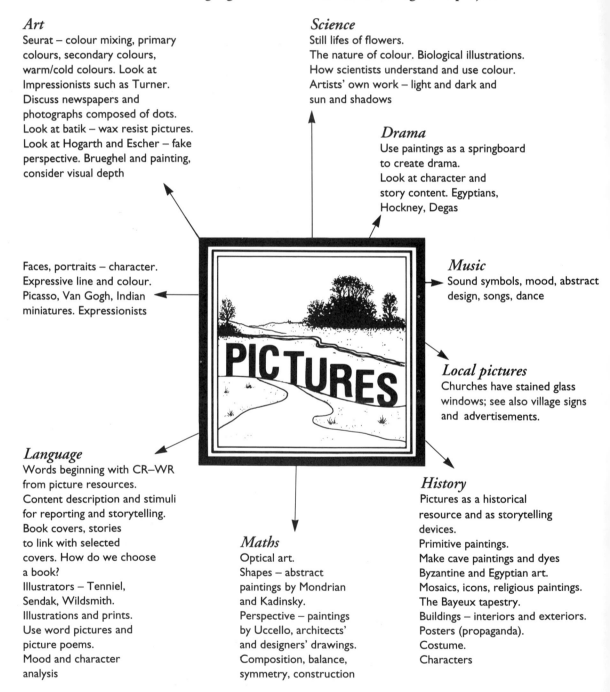

Art
Seurat – colour mixing, primary colours, secondary colours, warm/cold colours. Look at Impressionists such as Turner. Discuss newspapers and photographs composed of dots. Look at batik – wax resist pictures. Look at Hogarth and Escher – fake perspective. Brueghel and painting, consider visual depth

Science
Still lifes of flowers.
The nature of colour. Biological illustrations.
How scientists understand and use colour.
Artists' own work – light and dark and sun and shadows

Drama
Use paintings as a springboard to create drama.
Look at character and story content. Egyptians, Hockney, Degas

Faces, portraits – character. Expressive line and colour. Picasso, Van Gogh, Indian miniatures. Expressionists

Music
Sound symbols, mood, abstract design, songs, dance

Local pictures
Churches have stained glass windows; see also village signs and advertisements.

Language
Words beginning with CR–WR from picture resources. Content description and stimuli for reporting and storytelling. Book covers, stories to link with selected covers. How do we choose a book? Illustrators – Tenniel, Sendak, Wildsmith. Illustrations and prints. Use word pictures and picture poems. Mood and character analysis

Maths
Optical art.
Shapes – abstract paintings by Mondrian and Kadinsky.
Perspective – paintings by Uccello, architects' and designers' drawings.
Composition, balance, symmetry, construction

History
Pictures as a historical resource and as storytelling devices.
Primitive paintings.
Make cave paintings and dyes Byzantine and Egyptian art. Mosaics, icons, religious paintings. The Bayeux tapestry.
Buildings – interiors and exteriors. Posters (propaganda).
Costume.
Characters

Some projects sub-divide very easily into different subject areas of the National Curriculum. In the wood project outlined below, ideas focusing on specific areas of the curriculum are listed. It would be possible to focus on any one of these as a way into the project.

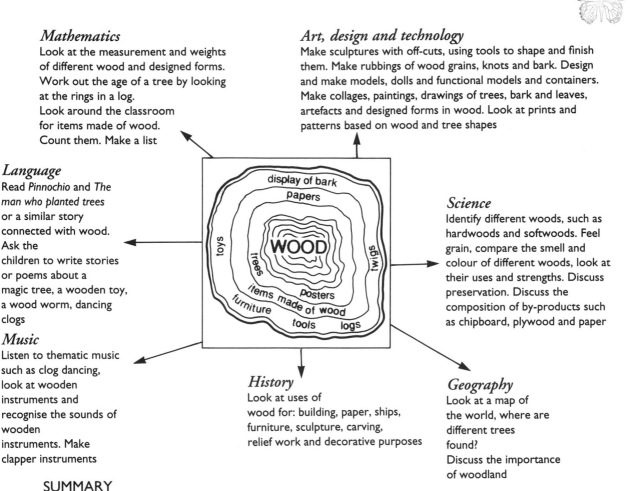

Mathematics

Look at the measurement and weights of different wood and designed forms. Work out the age of a tree by looking at the rings in a log. Look around the classroom for items made of wood. Count them. Make a list

Language

Read *Pinnochio* and *The man who planted trees* or a similar story connected with wood. Ask the children to write stories or poems about a magic tree, a wooden toy, a wood worm, dancing clogs

Music

Listen to thematic music such as clog dancing, look at wooden instruments and recognise the sounds of wooden instruments. Make clapper instruments

Art, design and technology

Make sculptures with off-cuts, using tools to shape and finish them. Make rubbings of wood grains, knots and bark. Design and make models, dolls and functional models and containers. Make collages, paintings, drawings of trees, bark and leaves, artefacts and designed forms in wood. Look at prints and patterns based on wood and tree shapes

Science

Identify different woods, such as hardwoods and softwoods. Feel grain, compare the smell and colour of different woods, look at their uses and strengths. Discuss preservation. Discuss the composition of by-products such as chipboard, plywood and paper

History

Look at uses of wood for: building, paper, ships, furniture, sculpture, carving, relief work and decorative purposes

Geography

Look at a map of the world, where are different trees found? Discuss the importance of woodland

SUMMARY

In the non-statutory guidance for the National Curriculum for art and design, it is stated that within the specific requirements of the programmes of study there is sufficient flexibility for teachers and pupils to follow their particular interests.

With experience of the whole range of curriculum requirements it will be possible to fulfil a number of attainment targets for different disciplines from particular themes and projects. This underlines the value of working from a central stimulus using both pre-planned and open-ended modes of teaching and learning.

5 Creating displays – the ways and the means

There are, of course, a number of basic practical requirements which one needs to consider in the context of learning how to develop better environments and displays in your school, and the first consideration must be the materials and tools for the job. I have therefore compiled a list in the first part of this chapter, outlining the most important materials. This is followed by a section which I hope will provide some insights for those who are less experienced in the skills required for the mounting and display of two- and three-dimensional work; it offers guidance in regard to basic equipment and furniture and the problems encountered in lettering.

ESSENTIAL MATERIALS

Basic paper requirements

It is important to make sure that your school has a wide variety of paper and card for both work and display purposes. There is a need for a basic range of sugar paper, cartridge paper and newsprint of various qualities. Black, white and neutral ranges are especially useful for setting-off work which is to be mounted and presented but some strong hues are also necessary. Paper can be acquired from manufacturers and firms specialising in art materials but there are also other fruitful sources where paper can be obtained for little cost. Local printers, packaging firms and businesses can sometimes offer offcuts and newspaper printers often sell remaindered rolls which are too short for a print run, at very reasonable prices.

The following list is of some of the types of paper which you may wish to incorporate into your displays and outlines some of the characteristics, properties and usage of these papers.

- Cartridge paper – choose a variety of sizes and qualities. This is a basic drawing paper for pencil, paint or inks.
- Sugar paper – can be used either for mounting or for painting. It comes in two main types: neutral colours such as black, grey and buff or in bright colours which are used for displaying work which can be effectively enhanced, such as written work. It is important to note that sugar paper fades in strong light and should only be used for short-term displays. If it is required for use in longer-term displays, try plasticising it with watered down PVC glue – at a ratio of two-thirds glue to one-third water. This should slow down the fading process.
- Bank and bond paper – these are thin, smooth-surfaced drawing or writing paper.
- Newsprint or kitchen paper – this is off-white porous paper. It is excellent for brush work, paint, print and some drawings. It is also a good paper for experimenting.
- Tissue, cellophane and rolls of coloured paper – these can often be reused more than once for backing purposes, or will enhance dull wall surfaces.
- Corrugated card – this can be used in various heights and colours and is useful for creating bays and backgrounds, or covering boxes, tables and stools (see figure 27 on page 64). Coloured corrugated card is much more expensive than the buff and is inclined to fade.
- Rolls of narrow strip paper – these come in varying widths from 2 to 20 centimetres and they are used for creating the outlines of shapes, framing work and for breaking up large areas of board into sections. Any strip-offcuts created when trimming work on the paper cutter or guillotine should be saved: they are useful for framing or for weaving.
- Crepe paper – this can be cut into block shapes or strips to create attractive edging.
- Card – this may be used for specialist mounting or making letter forms. If card is used as a mount it is possible to pin or lightly staple work to it rather than gluing it, thus enabling it to be used again.

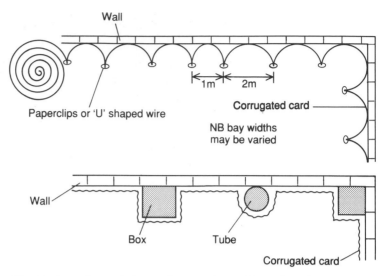

Figure 27   Card may be stapled on to boxes, tubes, tables and stools

Adhesives

Adhesives are obviously used extensively in display work, but it is extremely important to remember that Health and Safety Regulations state that some adhesives may not be used by children. It is necessary to read any labels or descriptive material carefully before making any purchase.

Likewise one needs to choose an appropriate glue for the weight and strength of the materials being used. There is nothing more frustrating than spending hours displaying work to find that it is hanging off its background the following day. The following list outlines a number of suitable glues for school display work:

- PVA glue – this is ideal for most materials, as it is strong enough for collage materials including heavy materials such as pieces of wood, yet when watered down, it is light enough for even the most delicate materials.
- Wallpaper adhesives – these are ideal for covering boards when you have a more permanent display material in mind, such as hessian or bookbinding fabrics. Some manufactures sell board-sized off-cuts of hessian at a fraction of the cost of lengths bought by the metre.

- Copydex – this is an excellent glue for fabrics, card and paper products.
- Wood glues – these are specifically designed to hold materials which contract and expand. They are only necessary when joining larger pieces of material. Otherwise PVA glues are adequate for all smaller items.
- Impact adhesives – these may be used by children under close adult supervision for bonding heavy duty materials but children need to be taught to follow instructions carefully.

Fabrics

Fabrics are undoubtedly valuable and versatile display materials and virtually any interesting lengths which can be draped or stretched are valuable assets for display. Cotton, linen, wool, silk, chiffon, polyester, viscose and other manufactured fabrics, nets and laces are all useful to have as alternative background materials to paper or card. All of these materials may be purchased in a variety of lengths and a stock can be built-up over a number of years. Samples, offcuts, and ends-of-rolls in both the dress and furnishing departments of shops are worth looking at but jumble sales are often the best place to pick up fabrics at bargain prices.

Plain fabrics are usually more versatile than patterned, as they tend to enhance the subject matter better by not distracting the eye. However, there are some lovely textured and patterned fabrics which may be very effective if carefully balanced within a display.

Fabrics can also be displayed for their own qualities, rather than as backdrops for other items. They can be used to illustrate cultural variations in fabric-based art such as: Javanese batik, Scottish plaids, Indian prints, American patchwork and South American weaving. They can also be displayed for their scientific interests. Natural fabrics such as cotton, silk or linen could also be displayed as could their sources and processing methods. Manufactured fabrics could be displayed as a contrast. Fabrics can also be displayed to illustrate a technological point or craft-skills such as screen or roller printing, weaving, bonding or felting.

I have found it a very worthwhile experience to challenge and enable children to work using techniques such as batik, tie-dye, screen-printing or weaving. When presented in their own right, they offer a very good basis for cross-curricular work, and involve a wide selection of skills, including humanities, maths and language experience. It can be an ideal starting point for a whole project.

SCHOOL DISPLAY TOOL KIT

There are a number of basic tools which are essential for the practical business of creating good displays. It is useful to have sets of these tools placed strategically around the school where people can be sure of finding them to support their display needs at all times. Many teachers choose to have their own set which would of course be the ideal situation.

Suggested contents

- Staple gun – this is needed for stapling heavy duty materials and semi-permanent fixtures.
- Small stapler – this is adequate for most materials. Some fold to allow for use as both a hand- or wall-stapler.
- Staple remover – these are invaluable time-saving devices.
- Staples – these are clearly a useful means of fixing but can be a menace if driven too deeply into the board surface as they appear to resist all attempts at extraction. One solution is to attach a matchstick to the underside of your staple gun vent with sellotape. This stops the staples from being driven into the board too deeply. Alternatively, holding the staple gun at a slight angle leaves enough space to lever the staples out. It is important to clear the board completely of staples when dismantling a display as any left standing proud can cause injury to children.
- Rampin or pinpush – this is a tool to insert straight dressmaker or panel-pins into boards or similar surfaces.
- Pins – these need to be at least 3 cm long. They must also be used discreetly where young children are concerned but they are very effective when displaying fabrics, or thick materials such as card, rope and leather.

- Dressmaker's-pins – these are ideal for holding work on to pin-boarded walls. It is important to angle the pins point inward from the corners of the work in order to hold the paper or card flat. If angled into the board, wood, or hardboard panels, work can be held in place without being pierced. It is important to purchase stainless steel pins, as cheaper varieties will rust and damage the material which they hold. Dressmaker's-pins should not be placed in boards against which children can lean, or at children's head level.
- Panel-pins – these are stronger and thicker than dressmaker's-pins, and are capable of securing tougher and heavier materials.
- Mapping-pins – these are round-headed pins, sold in black, white, grey or bright colours. They are particularly useful when fastenings cannot be hidden, as they become a feature of the display.
- Drawing-pins – these are ideal for holding items in place but can damage the materials they hold and detract from the display if they are positioned too visibly. To avoid making holes in paper or card, push the pin into the board but not through the paper, catching the edge of the paper under the lip of the drawing-pin.
- Blu-tac – I recommend the use of Blu-tac for areas where there is no pinboard and where surfaces are tough such as where there is gloss or eggshell paint. It is also suitable for stopping three-dimensional items from slipping.
- Masking tape – this has many uses but its best quality is that it peels off surfaces more easily than other forms of sticky tape. All tapes and fastenings should be concealed whenever possible on displays.
- Double-sided tape – this is ideal for invisibly joining two or more materials.
- Strong, fine twine, thread, cord, nylon, or fishing line – these are particularly useful for suspending, tying, or linking items together.
- Fine wire – this is used to support or suspend fairly heavy items, too weighty for twine or thread.

- Paper-clips – these are particularly useful for holding paper, card and fabrics in place and for holding moulded material in shape.
- Paper-fasteners – these are a useful means of holding materials loosely together if flexibility is required.
- Adhesives – see page 64 for a detailed account of suitable adhesives for paper, card, wood, fabrics and metal.
- Pencils – these are used for marking out.
- Chalk – this is for general purposes and for use with string on a 'ping line' to create a horizontal or vertical guideline. (See figure 28 on page 69).
- Pens – your pack should include fine-line markers and square- or chisel-ended pens for lettering.
- Pliers – these are a very useful addition to any tool kit.
- Scissors – large dressmaker's scissors are required for the cutting of fabrics and other fine materials whilst large, heavy-duty, general-purpose scissors are needed for cutting paper, card and fairly tough materials. Fine dissecting scissors are suitable for delicate work such as cutting-out lettering and for complicated shapes. (Scissors of this kind are often found in the science section of order catalogues.)
- Pinking shears – these are useful for stopping the edges of fabric fraying and for creating decorative edges.
- Knives – these are for cutting-out and scoring activities.
- Retractable craft knife – this is particularly valuable for cutting intricate shapes in tough materials.
- Fine craft knife – this is for use in the delicate cutting of intricate shapes.
- Steel straight edge – this is like a ruler but doesn't necessarily have measurements marked on it. It is particularly useful for use in cutting a straight line, as unlike a wooden or plastic ruler it cannot be scored or damaged by the knife.
- Retractable tape measure – this is an indispensible item.
- Tool box – for ease of mobility, the above items may be stored in a sturdy tool box, preferably one with compartments. Any good DIY store will have a number of styles available and most at a reasonable cost.

> • Large paper or card cutter – this is an indispensible item for trimming and cutting work. It is advisable to buy the largest size, as you are bound to have fairly large-scale items to cut at some time. It is important that these are used and handled correctly if they are to last any length of time, so always follow the manufacturer's instructions carefully. Cutting wheels can be replaced when they become blunt. Of course, all cutting equipment must conform to current Health and Safety Regulations. Guillotines require safety guards.

Ping Line

- Measure the wall at both ends (or wherever required) to determine the required height of the ping line.
- Rub chalk along the string (the chalk should be a contrasting colour to the wall).
- Hold string against the wall at the required height and pull it tight.
- Pull the centre of the string as far away from wall as tension will allow, as with a bow string.
- Let go of the string at the centre. The string will ping against the wall leaving a chalk line, at the required height.

Figure 28   A ping line needs three people to work it

MOUNTING TWO-DIMENSIONAL WORK FOR DISPLAY PURPOSES

Creating attractive and informative displays requires skilful presentation of material and that involves careful and creative mounting. There are no hard and fast rules about mounting work, except that the major priority is to present the content in the best and most straightforward manner. The mount should sensitively enhance the material rather than contrast with it and the use of space is a key factor. Simplicity is of the utmost importance, not only in regard to the needs of the work or resource which is being displayed, but also in terms of the teacher's time.

The following guidelines were devised in order to help teachers to focus on the basic problems:

- Keep it simple.
- Attempt a clean-cut professional effect.
- Use neutral, enhancing colours and tones.
- Consider the proportional arrangement of space around items as well as the item itself.
- Minimise the use of appropriate adhesives.
- Always be aware of Health and Safety Regulations and fire risk legislation.

Any work which is displayed should always be presented clearly and crisply. Possibly the most important way of doing this is through the sensitive use of colour and tone. If the work to be displayed is delicate, or fairly neutral from a distance, mounts which are of some tonal contrast and which will draw the eye towards the work are effective. In contrast, brightly coloured items generally need fairly neutral colours to complement them. All work should have adequate breathing space, but 'busy' items really do need wide surrounds, as this provides space to hold the contents in focus.

It is useful to note that work does not have to be permanently fixed on to the mount. It can be placed for immediate effect (as in a temporary floor display, see page 37), or pinned. Both methods allow for the same mount to be used on a number of occasions.

Single mounting

This is the simplest method of enhancing work and proportion is the key to its success. The work needs a reasonably wide mount to isolate it from its surroundings if it is displayed as an individual piece. If it is to be placed with others to create a panel or composite picture, a narrower mount will suffice.

It is usual to 'lift' the content on the mount by giving the bottom margin a greater depth, as equal margins top and bottom give the optical illusion of dropping toward the bottom of the page. The side margins are optional in proportion, but are often equal to the top margin. The arrangement for written work, or a mixture of writing and illustrative matter, should conform to the same proportions.

Double mounting

When double mounting (that is using two mounts – one inner and one outer), the inner and outer margin can be of contrasting tones and the outer margin is often wider. The recommended proportions are the same as for single mounts, that is, equal top and side margins but a deeper bottom margin.

Window mounting

This consists of 'windows' or frames being cut from card or strong paper and placed over the work. It has the advantage of one being able to use the frame a number of times, but these windows or frames take time to produce and need to be measured and cut accurately. A quick alternative to this is to use torn 'window frames' which can be any irregular shape torn out of the centre of paper or card, and again placed over the work. These can be very effective.

The practice of cutting closely around work is not one that I would advocate, as in most cases it detracts from the pictures and does not take into consideration the child's chosen use of space.

Using adhesives on mounts

When glueing mounts, it is important to choose one with little or no water content as the paper is inclined to wrinkle. The same effect is caused by using too much adhesive. Teachers and children should both aim to use the minimum amount to serve its required purpose. The alternative to glueing is, of course, pinning or stapling, which have the advantage of allowing the mount to be used again.

The arrangement of two-dimensional work on panels or walls

The human mind longs for simplicity and goes to great lengths to assimilate information from the world around it in an understandable form. Making sense of our surroundings is a major part of our life-skill. We are greatly aided in our struggle to assimilate information if work can be arranged so that all horizontals and verticals are aligned wherever possible, thus making the content easier for the mind to take in. It is very important that we consider children's eye-levels if we are to communicate effectively.

I am convinced that work should be displayed at the same angle, and the same way up as it was when it was created, as it may have been the express desire of the artist to create it that way. I also believe that to angle or place items edge-to-edge (unless creating a panel), or to trim close to the contour is essentially disrespectful of the material and is failing to accept the content for what it is: an individual, personal statement, which should be seen as it was intended by the artist and in the way which human beings normally look at things! There are of course exceptions, for example, in the case of pattern making for fabric designs, but such displays have specific laws of their own.

Figure 29(a)   An interesting use of tone to display children's work based on a stuffed owl. Items can be attached lightly on to mounts, allowing for use in other contexts

Figure 29(b) Prints arranged to form an irregular shape. This method can prove useful when displaying around objects, or archways, doors and windows

Figure 29(c) Backing paper placed to create simple tonal shapes in contrast with the board. Work is then arranged within the suggested spaces

When dealing with a large number of diverse items it is sometimes a useful idea to divide the wall-board surfaces into geometric shapes by means of strips and sheets of paper and card. This gives structure to the surface and allows for a simplified grouping of items. Rectangles and squares are particularly effective, although circles and triangles can also be useful. The organisation can be symmetrical or irregular, or rhythmic divisions can be made by means of vertical bands or sheets of paper, card or fabric.

Figure 30(a,b above and opposite)   Two examples of 'busy' pictures enhanced by the use of coloured paper blocks in a contrasting tone

One technique is to place sheets of paper in selected positions on a panel, thus creating blocks of colour or tone and then using the spaces formed by these sheets for displaying work. These spaces act as frames and often the works displayed need no mount at all.

By breaking up boards in this manner the blocks, strips, or coloured sheets act as a guide to line up the work. It can also look very good before the work is displayed, which allows for a display to be slowly built-up without fear of leaving an eyesore prior to its completion. Leaving alternate areas free can actually enhance a display.

I have also found that if I have irregular shapes to display, I need to think of the overall effect almost as a jig-saw puzzle with shapes interlocking but not necessarily touching. I sometimes confine these shapes within an overall irregular shape, see figure 31 on page 76. To

Figure 30(b)

produce a stronger design it is usually better if the larger shapes are placed centrally, with the smaller ones graded around them. Alternatively, you could begin with large shapes to one side, tailing off to the smallest ones opposite. However, it is important that the work being presented controls the decisions which are made.

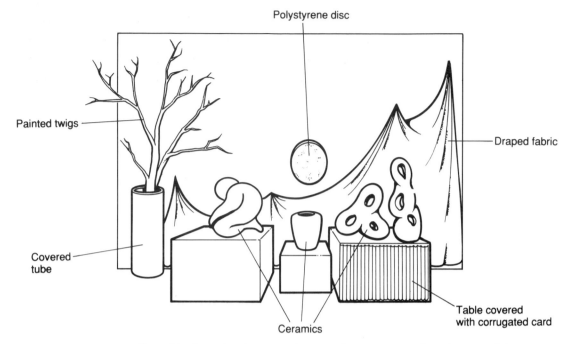

Figure 31   Irregular shapes need to complement one another, almost as if they are jig-saw pieces with space in between

The general rule when searching for simplicity is to respect and keep within the framework of the wall-board or chosen display area but there are, of course, always exceptions to the rule.

SURFACES FOR TWO-DIMENSIONAL PRESENTATION

Pin-boards

There are, of course, many types of surface on which displays can be erected but pin-boards and screens are two of the most important in schools. The use of pin-boards hung on walls and doors in working areas, allows for the maximum utilisation of space. In some schools where wall space was at a minimum and large expanses of glass existed in a classroom or corridor, we sometimes used battens across window frames on which pin-boards could be fixed or hung, at children's eye-level. Pin-boards are available in a wide range of materials, styles, sizes and costs. They should be selected for their neutral appearance and good quality surface which can take dressmaker's-, mapping- and drawing-pins as well as staples. Surfaces which only take velcro fixing can be very limiting in the long run. Boards should also have neat, strong edging which will not fray or pull away from the frame.

Screens

Screens are a necessary and versatile resource within a school. They allow for bays to be created and for areas to be divided and can be used either singly or as complex units.

Many styles are available but they differ a great deal in quality and most of them are expensive. You need to compare them carefully before making a final decision on what type and style is most suitable for your school's purposes. The following considerations may help as a guideline when choosing screens.

- Balance – screens which are too lightweight can be a danger, as they may overbalance but on the other hand those which are too heavy and cumbersome may deter people from using them, unless they are to stay mainly in one area. Take your own school's characteristics into account when choosing.
- Easy manoeuvrability – some sets of screens have castors. It is worth looking at the ones which lock when in position, specially if heavy screens have been selected.
- Linking system – screens can be linked together into units. It is important to have strong links which can be easily adjusted and they should be replaceable. A complicated system can take about four people to put one section together so go for simplicity!
- Durability – screens need to stand up to hard wear over the years. Weak material will twist and bend, resulting in badly aligned boards. The surface material, like that of pin-boards, should be neutral, durable and able to take a number of different fixings.

RESOURCES FOR THREE-DIMENSIONAL DISPLAY

As with two-dimensional displays there are particular qualities and requirements for displaying three-dimensional objects. In particular these objects need to be displayed on different levels if items are to be presented and enjoyed as individual pieces.

Boxes and stands

A set of boxes made in various sizes, and painted black, white or neutral tones will be an asset for any display area. If colour is required, these same boxes can be covered with paint, paper, plastic, leather or fabric.

When we could not afford to have these items professionally made, we always tried to find someone who would take pity on us and make a set of boxes out of wood, plywood, hardboard or a similar material. (Chipboard however is not really suitable for these items, as it tends to crumble after being in use for a while, even when laminated and it is also very heavy.) It is always worth trying to find a volunteer, who might also be willing to sand and paint them in order to help the school by providing such a valuable resource! Once made, such boxes will last for years. Obviously, the more you have, the more permutations are possible (see figure 32 opposite). It helps to simplify the storage of such a resource, if the boxes are made to fit inside one another. A set may then be built-up over a number of years.

There are also many excellent and clean shaped boxes in polystyrene or cardboard produced for supermarkets and radio, television and electrical shops. If painted and/or covered, these can make superb units at little or no cost.

Tubes or tins

When covered with paper, fabric or card, particularly corrugated card, tins or tubes can be made into really professional looking display resources and they cost little or nothing to make. It is however, very important to finish off such items well. Sanding rough surfaces, edges and corners, tucking in frayed ends and making sure materials meet edge-to-edge will make all the difference to the final appearance.

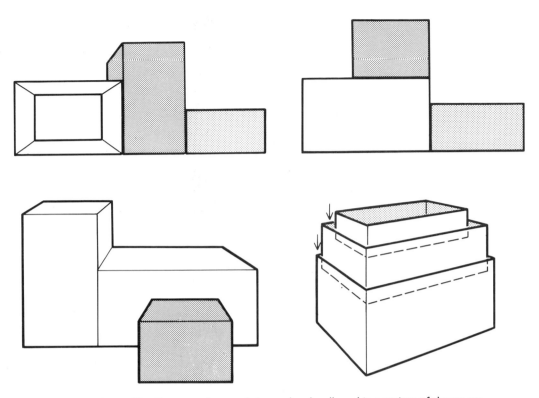

Figure 32   Boxes made out of plywood or hardboard in a variety of shapes are invaluable for display purposes. They can be made to be stored one inside the other

Stands

I have found free-standing wire display-stands such as those used for displaying books in libraries and bookshops particularly useful, specially when exhibiting flat ceramic pieces. These stands support objects and allow them to be displayed in an upright, or slightly angled position. You can find these items in many catalogues, under the library section. They can be bought a few at a time over a number of years, until a supply has been built-up. Better still, ask some older children to take on the challenge of producing stands as a technology project, which would be a good exercise in liaison, as well as in technology!

Shelves

All schools need shelving for a wide variety of storage and display functions but not least for the presentation of children's work. Metal tracking with adjustable brackets allows for versatile usage. If the wall area behind the tracking is pin-boarded there is the possibility of integrating wall and shelving displays using different configurations, and varying the proportions (see figure 33 below.) Alternatively one could use only the wall surface, or only the shelves. Tracking is also useful in window enclosures and recesses as items are not only protected by the recess, but are set-off to advantage by the daylight behind them. Translucent objects placed in this way are particularly valuable as visual stimuli.

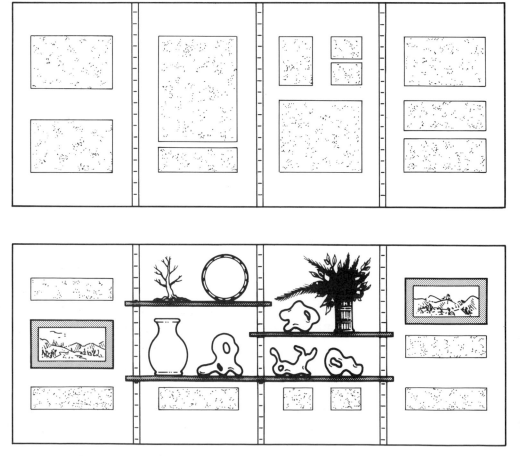

Figure 33   Shelves and pin-boards can be combined to make attractive display areas

Lighting

Wherever you present work or resources the display objects need to be seen clearly and the sensitive positioning of displays in relation to daylight, doors, windows, glass walls, or even small shafts of light needs consideration. Special lighting is expensive and therefore it needs careful research to find the best deal to fulfil all your needs. Once installed it should not incur too many maintenance costs, other than the occasional replacing of bulbs. (It is well worth costing the bulbs when making your pre-purchase enquiries about fittings.)

Spotlight tracking systems are amongst the most popular and versatile lighting systems. Their particular quality is their manoeuvrability which should allow you to illuminate most of your targeted areas. There is a wide variety of choice in regard to size and power, whilst the tracks themselves are fixed to either ceilings or walls and are therefore placed horizontally or vertically according to what is most suitable for the area.

Alternatively, fluorescent strip lights can be used, these are economical and suitable for concealed lighting which gives a softer effect. It is also useful to have free-standing spotlights available for lower-angled lighting. These may already be owned by your school for use in drama productions. The possibility of using coloured gels and shadow as an integral part of the display is an exciting idea to explore. Children can learn much about the nature of form, space, shadow, and light, including the mixing of coloured lights, when working with a teacher in this context.

Safety

Lastly, although it isn't actually a display resource, I recommend the purchase of a tray trolley. This is a useful aid which eases the mobilisation of materials between display areas. It is also as well to note that anything made by volunteer-helpers must be checked for safety and for the use of suitable materials such as non-toxic paint and rust-free nails and screws. All display items and resources must have smooth edges, surfaces and corners and no equipment should sport anything which is likely to cut or trap children. Of course, Health and Safety Regulations must always be adhered to.

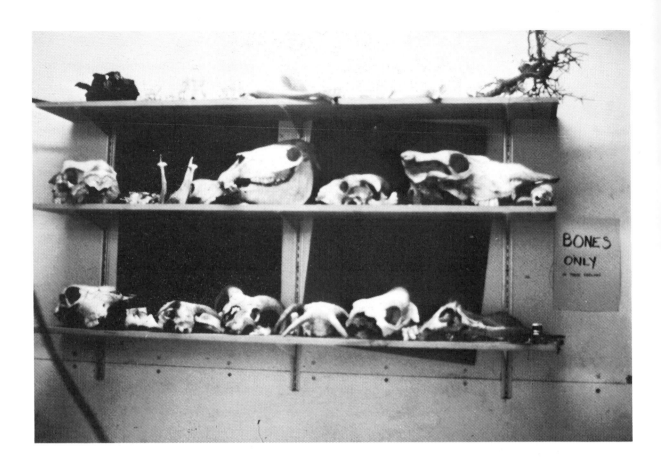

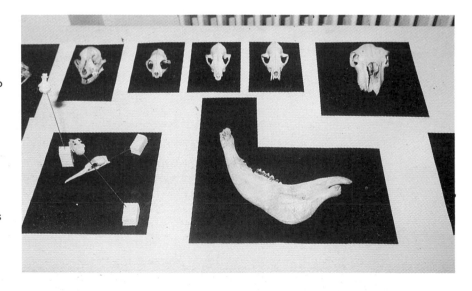

Figure 34(a)   Bones and skulls arranged on shelving. Note the dark paper placed between the shelves to enhance the light shapes

Figure 34(b)   The same bones and skulls placed on sheets of black paper and arranged to give a clear visual impact

Figure 34(a,b,c,d)   Good display is built on effective use of space. In most cases items need to be seen clearly and look uncluttered

Figure 34(c,d) Adjustable shelving can be used in entrances, libraries, narrow recesses or classrooms, to display three-dimensional items including books. This kind of shelving allows for many different combinations and uses. The tracking may be fitted to a wall or board and flat displays placed over them when supports and shelves are not in use

Figure 34(c)

Figure 34(d)

Figure 35(a,b)   (opposite and above) Many older buildings have old open lockers or shelving which can be utilised in resource areas with a little paint and/or washable plastic. They can be used for storing items of interest which children have brought into school as well as more permanent collections. Objects may be easily rearranged, or replaced when used in other areas of the school

Figure 36(a)   A nursery environment where children are encouraged to develop organisation skills. Each area of the room has a specific purpose, enabling equipment and materials to be easily found. Display also has a high priority in this school as is obvious from this picture

Figure 36(b)   Nursery work extended into the corridor

LETTERING AND VISUAL COMMUNICATION

The importance of lettering

The whole business of lettering needs to be considered when planning any learning environment as it is obviously a major form of communication. If written information is necessary it should be clear and effective, enhancing rather than detracting from the presentation.

There are three fundamental uses of lettering for visual communication in schools. The first is the immediate response, where the teacher needs to make a point, add a label, put up a spelling or interact with a child. The second is the teacher's pre-planned presentation in relation to the resource and the third is the child's own written communication as he/she acts and reacts to stimuli or labels and explains his/her collection or work. All three are an inherent and valuable part of display work.

An ability to communicate in words is, of course, a fundamental skill for any teacher and child. The quality of a teacher's spoken communication plays a major part in our children's learning process and in one sense, the written communication incorporated into the teaching resource (which is used to label, explain or challenge) is an extension of this educational conversation. So too is the teacher's response to a child's display work as the work progresses. Therefore both the labelling and written work on the display and our responses to a child's work, need to be of a high quality and a sensitive nature.

Children's own lettering

It is as well to think ahead when children's written work is to be presented. Encourage them to choose tools which make strong marks, whether they are pencils or pens. The paper should be smooth and white for normal usage, although white writing on black paper can be very effective and pale hues of paper are exciting for specific projects. Let the children use grids if you feel that they need them. Even a lined piece of file paper will work as a guide behind bank or bond paper. The inclusion of margins on either side of the grid makes a great difference in the visual communication, as it isolates the work and makes it easily readable.

Teacher's lettering

Initially, it is very important to decide on a basic alphabet which is reasonably formed and unembellished for use throughout the school. It should bear some relationship to the letter forms and numbers in the reading scheme, and all members of staff, ancilliary helpers and others who assist in the classroom should be given a copy.

Figure 37(a,b,c)
Examples of lettering produced by student teachers. Grids can be used as a guideline in the same way as one would when using a writing pad

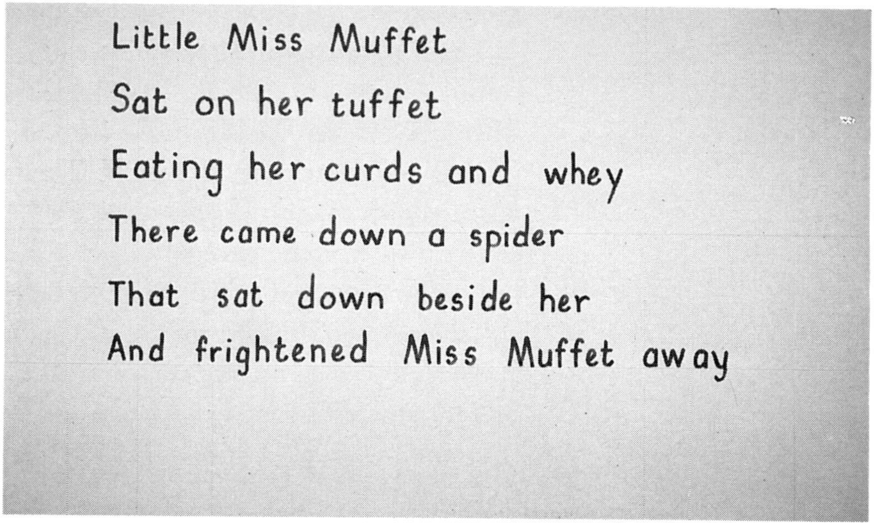

> Little Miss Muffet
> Sat on her tuffet
> Eating her curds and whey
> There came down a spider
> That sat down beside her
> And frightened Miss Muffet away

Figure 37(a)   Lettering with a round-ended nib is usually easier for left-handed people to use. It produces strokes of a uniform thickness as seen in this example

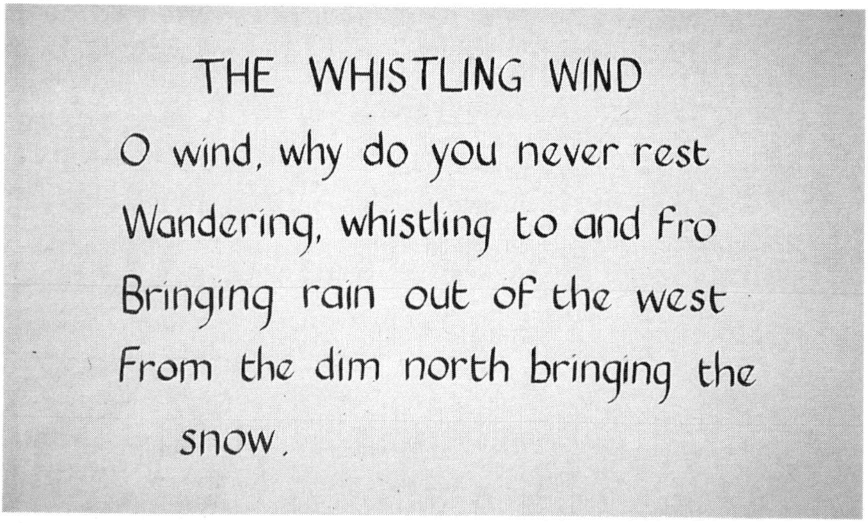

> THE WHISTLING WIND
> O wind, why do you never rest
> Wandering, whistling to and fro
> Bringing rain out of the west
> From the dim north bringing the
> snow.

Figure 37(b)   Lettering illustrating the use of a chisel-pointed nib held at forty-five degrees

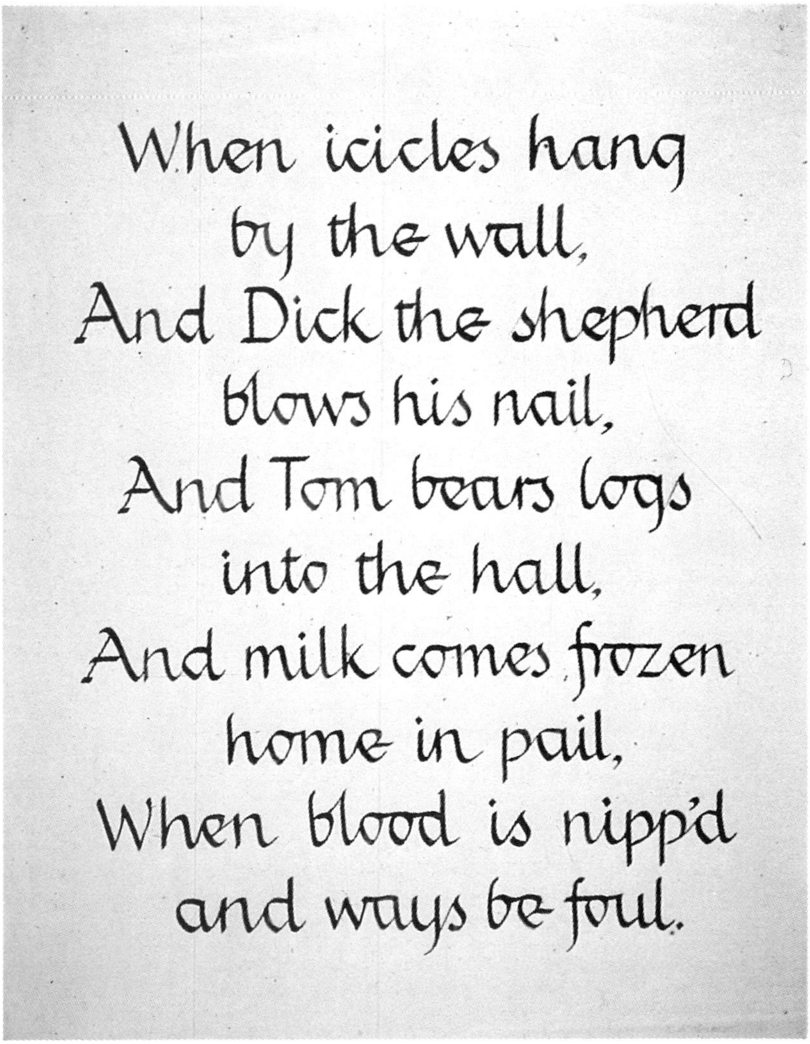

When icicles hang
by the wall,
And Dick the shepherd
blows his nail,
And Tom bears logs
into the hall,
And milk comes frozen
home in pail,
When blood is nipp'd
and ways be foul.

Figure 37(c)   It is sometimes useful to practise writing letters with a wide italic or felt-tip pen. If the angle is a constant forty-five degrees it enables you to be consistent, and accentuates thick and thin lines

I have included a very basic model which I have found useful. It proved to be functional and not too intimidating. However, there are many excellent calligraphic models for schools who wish to base their lettering on a more sophisticated model.

If a staff member is already skilled in basic calligraphy, it would be useful if he/she were able to share this expertise and offer guidance on tools and techniques to other teachers. However, there is a need

Capitals 7 thick strokes of nib
Lower case 4½-5.

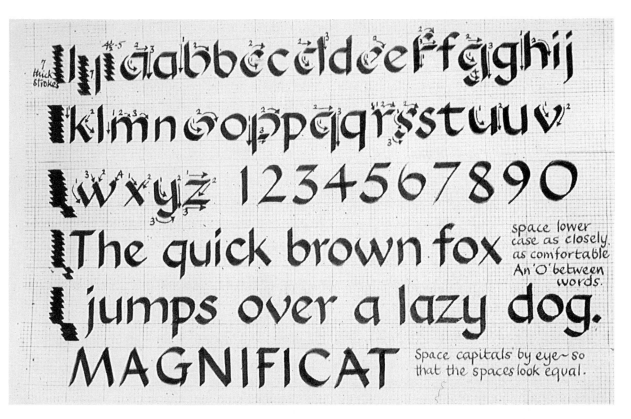

Figure 38(a,b) (opposite and above) Examples of upper- and lower-case letters which may be practiced to develop lettering skills

for all of us to make the most of our existing but unpractised skills as we look at techniques for direct pen, felt-tip or fibre-tip lettering. It is very interesting to see how staff who are willing to spend a couple of sessions considering lettering proportions, spacing and pen practice can improve quite dramatically in a short space of time.

A very simple set of upper- and lower-case letters are presented in figure 38a and b above and opposite in a sequence which enables the build up of certain skills and shapes. I would encourage you to practise them, repeating each line until you are satisfied, which is seldom at the first sitting, but may well be by the second. A grid can save the need for drawing out rules. It should preferably be made of card with lines drawn in black fibre-tip or biro thickly enough to act as a guide (in the same way as one uses the grid paper in a normal writing pad). Bank, bond, or any other thin white paper allows the lines to show through and used with pencil, pen and ink, or water-based felt-tips or fibre-tips can be a very useful aid. (Spirit-based pens mark through the paper on to the grid which is not to be recommended!) Finally, it is important to select good tools which make clean strong marks. Crayons and pencils will play a part, specially if children are also involved but most lettering will be done with pens.

Pens

Pens will need to be carefully selected. There are a wide choice of ink, water- or spirit-based pens for sale and each type has particular qualities and uses. Square- and chisel-ended felt-tips are popular and enable the writer to vary the thickness of his/her pen strokes. The use of a chisel-shaped tool allows for a pleasing effect of thick and thin strokes providing it is held at an angle of forty-five degrees and the angle remains constant throughout. However, some people, especially those who are left-handed, find that a round-ended felt-pen is a better tool for their needs. It is possible to cut the tip off cleanly and use it vertically. This results in lettering of a uniform thickness throughout.

Some of the cheaper felt-pens have poor quality tips which distort after a short time. As with many tools, the cheapest is not always the best buy in the long run. Manufacturers such as Berol, Platignum, Osmiroid, Steidler and Schreiber also produce sets of italic or similar calligraphy pens ranging in size. These are very good value and can be used by staff or older children.

The size of the lettering in relation to the tool you provide is critical. Even expert calligraphers who attempt large lettering with a small tool can come to grief, whilst the most amateur letterer using appropriate sized proportions can be surprised and delighted by the improvement in the quality of his/her work.

Alphabet templates

If large letters are required, one of the easiest ways to produce them is to make sets of the alphabet in various sizes and styles out of fairly strong card. These can be drawn round and cut out time and again (my sets lasted about ten years) using materials ranging from wallpaper to corrugated card. This really can give a professional look to the display, particularly if you spend time experimenting with the spacing before you stick them down. Obviously it takes some time to prepare the alphabets, but it is well worth the effort.

Computer generated lettering

For smaller lettering and labels which do not need to be hand written, why not use a computer? Many programmes provide a variety of typefaces which look neat and professional, particularly when printed in colour. Children can easily become involved in this activity which obviously widens the value of the exercise beyond art and display and into the information technology area of the curriculum. Word processors are often used to effect by children but it is just as important for them to achieve a good balance of text and space when using a computer as it is with handwritten work.

SUMMARY

Lettering and letter forms are functional parts of our world today. In our schools we need to consider the messages we transmit and the means by which we do it. In the final instance we must assess and evaluate the effectiveness of our communication and whether we have added to, or detracted from, our environment by the way in which we present it.

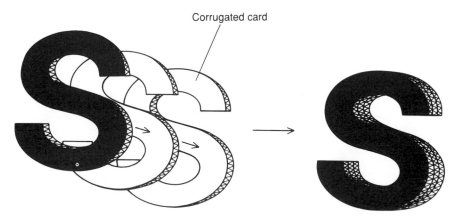

Corrugated card

Figure 39　If lettering is to play a prominent part in a display, three-dimensional letters can be made by gluing together a number of identical shapes cut out of thick or corrugated card. Different shadow effects can be created with strategically placed lighting

Conclusion

In 1981 Ernest Goodman, Chairman of the School's Council Art Committee, wrote the foreword to an excellent and timeless *Occasional Bulletin* titled 'Resources for Visual Education 7–13'. In his foreword he said that the dominant underlying principle expounded in the bulletin was one that he was sure all thoughtful teachers would approve, it stated that what was of:

> prime importance in the field [was] guided sensory stimulus of concrete experience and ample teacher–pupil dialogue rather than second- or third-hand images, contrived feeling and easy prescriptions.
>
> Goodman, 1981

In 1992 the National Curriculum Art documentation reinforced this view by requiring in its statutory programmes of study, that children should work from direct experience, that they should collect and sort images, objects and source materials and that they should look at and talk about examples of work by artists from a variety of periods and cultures.

We know that knowledge is imparted in many different ways but I believe that there is no educational stimulus quite like seeing the real item in the hands of a lively and enthusiastic teacher. I am sure you will agree that once one has worked in this way and systematically extended our children's education by enabling them to learn from this firsthand experience of their own, their peers and other people's work: it would be very difficult for anyone to convince us that there was a better way of teaching or learning.

Bibliography

Adam, E. and Ward, C. *Art and the Built Environment*, Harlow, Longman, 1982

Arnheim, R. *Art and Visual Perception*, London, Faber and Faber, 1967 (UK)
    Berkeley, University of California Press, 1974 (US)

Calouste Gulbenkian Foundation, *The Arts in Schools*, London, Oyez Press, 1982

Clement, R. *The Art Teacher's Handbook*, London, Hutchinson, 1985

Cotton, A. and Haddon, F. *Learning and Teaching Through Art and Craft*,
    London, Batsford, 1974

Department of Education and Science, *Art in the National Curriculum*, London,
    DES, 1992

Dixon, P. *Display in the Primary School*, Winchester, Peter Dixon Books 1985

Gentle, Keith. *Children and Art Teaching*, London, Croom Helm, 1985 (UK)
    New York, Routledge, Chapman & Hall, 1985 (US)

Leicester Education Committee. *Learning through Art*, Leicester, Leicester County
    Council, 1982

Makoff, J. and Duncan, L. *A World of Display*, London, Belair Publications, 1990

Morgan, Margaret. *Art 4–11. Art in the Early Years of Schooling*. Oxford, Basil
    Blackwell Ltd, 1988, and London, Simon Schuster, 1992

Pickering, J. *Visual Education in the Primary School*, London, Batsford, 1971

Read, H. *Education Through Art*, London, Faber and Faber, 1959

Schools Council Art Committee, *Resources for Visual Education 7–13*, Schools
    Council Publications, London, HMSO, 1981

Suffolk County Council, *Art 8–14. In the Middle Years of Schooling*, Suffolk
    Education Authority, Ipswich, 1981

Taylor, R. *Educating for Art*, Harlow, Longman, 1986

Colour section – art and design in practice

Figure C1(a)   Long corridors are prominent in most schools and can make buildings look institutional. Plants may be used effectively, to break up the long perspective

Figure C1(b)   One often sees narrow sections of wall jutting out into corridors. A narrow board placed on such a wall utilises an otherwise unused display space and shortens the elongated perspective of the corridor

Figure C1(c)   Consider utilising window sills or making hung arrangements

Figure C2(a)   Cloakroom areas are often neglected, yet if they are well organised and made to look interesting, they can become an integral part of the caring atmosphere of a school which influences children in the way that they respond to an environment

Figure C2(b)   A small recess leading to a storage cupboard has been effectively used to display books and create a quiet corner

Figure C2(c)   Wherever possible the outside environment of a school should be made as exciting and stimulating as the classroom. With a little imagination and planning, gardens and play areas can offer tremendous learning opportunities

Figure C3(a)   Screens and boxes have been used to create an alcove in a corridor. The design is strong, simple, and full of interest. This structure or one like it, could be used to present a wide variety of resources, collections and examples of children's work

Figure C3(b)   An alcove or window recess may be utilised to display a collection of interesting items. In this case red fabric has been draped over boxes and taken into the line of the window frame to enhance the white ceramics arranged on different levels. Without the tonal contrast created by the fabric it would not have been as effective

Figure C4(a)
A classroom where
children can work in an
interesting, well
organised environment

Figure C4(c)   A 'special unit'
area created by using screens
to section-off a working area
and provide a background to
display resource material

Figure C4(b)   Special
areas such as 'home
corners' encourage
practical and creative
development. The
decor may be changed
from time to time,
with the children
themselves making
suggestions and
carrying out their ideas
whenever possible

Figure C4(d)   A low-level blackboard is very useful for children to work out their own
ideas and it gives them great confidence

Figure C5(a)   This stained glass interior window reflects light into two of the classrooms in a small primary school in Suffolk. It was made by artist Surinder Warboys, and designed by her husband Roland. Money was raised for the commission through private donations, gifts from the parish council and private enterprise by the school

Figure C5(b)   A wall-hanging made by a high school pupil and borrowed by a primary school for children to work from

Figure C6(a)   Some schools provide areas where children may read or work quietly. This space has been transformed into a jungle scene, with children's work suspended from the ceiling to create atmosphere

Figure C6(b)   Children love to dress up, so why not use this enjoyment as a stimulus for creative work? Costumes may be borrowed from your drama department, or a local theatre group. Some may even be made up as you participate in the project, with lengths of fabric tied or pinned around the child. Screens, drapes or relevant items could be arranged as a background if needed. Work of this kind would, of course, have to be of a short duration for young children. Alternatively, a dummy or model may prove more successful, as it could be left and referred to again at a later date

Figure C7(a)   A mixed, primary group of children working inside a 'cave' made out of corrugated card, which has been set up in a corner of their classroom. They are using paints and dyes made by themselves from earth, berries and vegetables

Figure C7(b)   Outside their cave, there is a display of interesting and informative material for the children to use

Figure C8(a)   This classroom has been reorganised to allow the children to respond to a particular brief. Space has been created to allow for group and individual work to take place

Figure C8(b)   A school where the classroom is extended into the open-air whenever possible, with full use made of space and facilities

Figure C9(a)
Critical studies

Figure C9(b)
A series of textures
and mark-making
exercises made by
children aged
five- to seven-years,
after looking at, and
talking about, the
work of Van Gogh

Figure C10(a)   The painter Mondrian was the subject of this group of paintings by a reception class. The children looked at primary colours and the breaking up of space into segments and shapes

Figure C10(b)   Paintings based on the work of Rousseau by a group of mixed age primary children. This work was preceded by a discussion about jungles and animals. Stories and poems were read to excite the children's imaginations

Figure C11(a) and (b)   A project on water was developed in a number of directions from the initial brief to include language, art, science and technology. In figure C11(a) three-dimensional shapes and a screen placed at right angles help to extend the display work on the pin-board out into the surrounding area

Figure C12(a)   A mathematics display presented as a band of information with contrasting colour bands above and below to accentuate it

Figure C12(b)   This combined study of shape and pattern evolved in maths lessons. The small repeated patterns suggested forms which were taken into three-dimensions on a much larger scale. The forms were made in card and covered with foil but alternatively they could have been painted or covered with another material

Figure C12(c)   Wall-boards can be sectioned to create areas for specific information, or to sub-divide parts of a whole as can be seen in this mathematical display. Each shape has been given an allotted area, including hanging space, which combines with the other areas to create the complete environment

Figure C13(a,b,c)
These three displays
were the result of a
great deal of research
about the Ancient
Egyptians

Figure C13(b)   Large entrance areas lend themselves to this kind of display. The
mummified figure was made from modrock (plaster impregnated bandage) which the
children had great fun wrapping around the display model's limbs. They eventually
pieced sections together to form the whole body

Figure C13(a)   A wall
panel using a pin-board
to break up the long
perspective of a
corridor

Figure C13(c)   Death
masks designed and
made by children aged
nine- to ten-years

Figure C14(a) and (b) Overhead space can easily be forgotten as we tend to observe objects mainly at eye level. These mobile displays catch the eye because they are large and colourful

Figure C15(a) and (b)   Hanging pictures in this way creates immediate gallery space for children to assess their own and other's work. It also provides a suitable means of storing work while it dries

Figure C15(c)   When books are displayed they are usually meant to be read. This calls for special thought as the display must be functional. This is one answer. The display presents books on the painter Mondrian which children aged seven- to nine-years have made and wish to share. They are suspended on cord to create an unusual and creative display

Figure C16(a) A collection of surprise boxes, which have been given extra interest by being arranged as a wall display, thus producing a three-dimensional panel

Figure C16(b) This display shows a collage or painting, made up of individual units enabling all the class to take part in creating the finished whole. The infant children took part in arranging the units to their own satisfaction. Note the purpose for breaking the base line on this occasion

Figure C16(c) This is a good example of children building up individual units and arranging them to create a whole wall-panel. It is interesting to see how the display is extended by the use of overhead space

Figure C17(a)   The brief for this picture was to design and make a wall-hanging for a specific area at the end of a corridor in the school. The subject of the picture was 'Things of the sky'. The theme was chosen after a discussion about decorating the original tie-dye hanging. Children experimented with tie-dye roundels on smaller pieces of fabric before carrying them out on the larger wall-hanging

Figure C17(b)   This panel was covered with crisp packets, producing rich colours and textures. These may also be arranged in ranges of colour or tones to produce larger shapes relevant to pictures or patterns

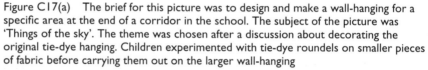

Figure C17(c)   Children aged nine to eleven in an art club, painted directly on to a hardboard panel which was fixed to a corridor wall. The design was based on the children's experience of Norwich market

Figure C18(a) and (b)   These paintings are part of a series about castles designed and created by groups of mixed aged primary children. The idea was to create atmosphere in a school hall to be used for language and drama work. Children love working on a large scale and learn to develop co-operative and organisational skills through group projects

Figure C19(a)   A symmetrical display about spring. The pictures are on single white mounts, echoing the plain white border frame of the board

Figure C19(b)   An example of individual units being grouped together to make a whole collection following the visit of a clown to the school

Figure C19(c)   A composite panel made from paintings about summer, without a mount in sight!

Figure C20(a) and (b)   These displays were used as resources for projects about building. Children had reference to actual building materials which were supported by pictures of buildings and structures. Both written and pictorial information is well balanced

Figure C20(c)   Building of a different kind! Children's pictures of birds' nests add interest to a display

Figure C20(d)   A display to celebrate the harvest season, where children have developed work from stimuli which they have brought into school. This needs to be well planned and executed as the display resources have a limited life

Figure C21(a) and (b) Individual and group work developed with Liz Rideal (Education Officer at the National Portrait Gallery) working as an artist in residence. Note the use of coloured blocks and strips of paper to create sections and frames for the pictures

Figure C21(c) Large boards may be separated into sections by means of coloured papers or strips. The brown sections in these illustrations are the original board, while paper forms blocks of colour. This background was used two or three times for different work

Figure C21(d) On occasion, to save time when mounting thicker collages and embroideries, I used wide strips of paper horizontally and vertically to create frames for the work

117

Figure C22(a) and (b)   A landscape created from tissue paper, dried plants, fabric and wood offcuts. It was built to inspire creative use of materials and resources

Figure C23   Part of a French project, where children borrowed, wrote for and collected relevant material to be displayed

Figure C24(a)   Some interesting book covers displayed to make children aware of graphic design for a future book project. The lettering was taken from an alphabet made in strong card and used as templates

Figure C24(b)   A group of magazine pictures forming a panel on the subject of natural forms. This was one of a series of panels, each depicting a different subject

Figure C25   Puppets arranged at different heights and balanced on boxes and tubes over which lengths of plain fabric have been draped. The semi-circular base was acquired from a department store which was replacing furniture and fittings. It has been used many times since. Note that the lettering is arranged to complement the display

Figure C26(a)

Figure C26(b)

Figure C26(d)

Figure C26(c)

Figure C26(a,b,c,d)   Environment and resources in a school for children with severe learning difficulties and profound and multiple learning difficulties, many of whom have additional sensory problems. The school staff have discussed, and worked out, a three year plan of whole year topics and themes, which form the basis for addressing the entire curriculum. Each department decides on an aspect of the theme to develop. These illustrations are examples of 'The world around us' project and show something of different cultures and places.

Display is crucial in any school with children who have learning difficulties for the promotion of language development and stimulation. It is an integral part of providing a broad and balanced curriculum. Much of the display in the school is initially staff led, owing to the children's problems. The staff collect items and also use the Education Authority's multi-cultural resource centre collection.

The 'Rainforest' idea was developed through colour and vision, feel, smells, and sounds, together with animal and plant forms. The whole combined to provide interest and stimulation to encourage learning skills. Many of the displays throughout the school are labelled in words and symbols

Figure C27(a)   The cat is framed by a torn irregular shaped window mount which has been placed over it

Figure C27(b)   There are times when children produce something really special. In such cases double mounting is worthwhile to communicate the content to its best effect

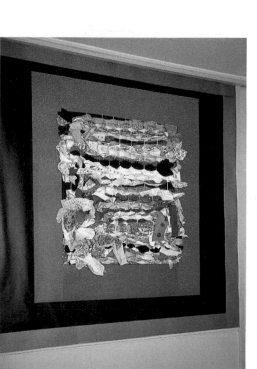

Figure C27(c)   Single mounted work is effective and functional, as in the case of this collage by a group of nine-year-olds. The mount frames should complement the picture while contrasting with the background

Figure C28(a,b,c)   A series of open boxes used to create individual units. They were draped with interesting fabrics to support a variety of objects. These were placed side by side and back to back to allow for all-round vision and for working purposes

Figure C29 (a,b)   Immediate resources are used to back up an idea, emphasise a point or to react to an active learning situation

Figure C29(a)   A collection of objects begged and borrowed from a local fishmarket to support a project

Figure C29(b)   Building materials collected to support a project

Figure C30(a) and (b)   Collected items of interest are brought into schools by children and staff to support specific learning purposes. Fabrics are used to soften and enhance these displays

Figure C31(a)   An interesting display of green items. The two- and three-dimensional artefacts are linked by soft lines of fabric

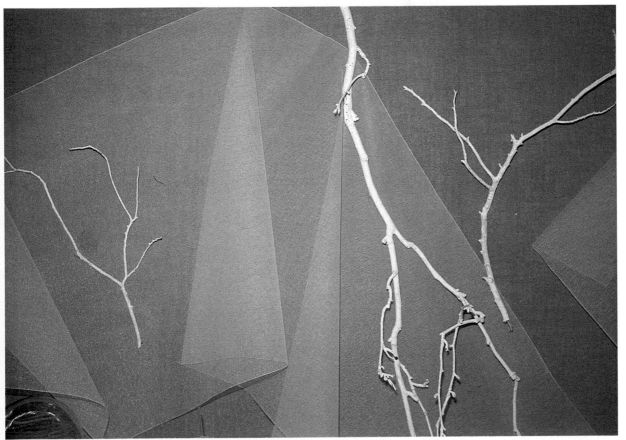

Figure C31(b)   Detail of a display in which painted twigs lie in the shapes created by draped fabric

Figure C32(a)   This display about the moon, was created to develop observation of tones and textures and suggest imaginative ideas. The use of bookbinding gauze creates tonal structures and the crumpled foil displays textures and reflections. Most of the space structures were made from tubes and household items. Large boxes and tables placed at different levels give added interest

Figure C32(b)   These corrugated bays show how it is possible to create sectional displays which combine to achieve a pleasing whole display. Varying the widths of the supports used to display artefacts adds to the displays interest